CONSIDER THE EVIDENCE

CONSIDER THE EVIDENCE

A Trial Lawyer Examines
Eyewitness Testimony
in Defense of the Reliability
of the New Testament

DANIEL P. BUTTAFUOCO

BEST GUESTS PRESS

Best Guests Press
9 Broadman Parkway
Jersey City, NJ 07305
201-432-7300
http://thebestguests.com/

Best
Guests
PRESS

Printed in the United States of America.

This book is based on a lecture originally given by Daniel P. Buttafuoco at the Billy Graham Evangelistic Association headquarters in Charlotte, North Carolina on May 28, 2015.

ISBN-13: 978-0-99738-774-2

This book is dedicated to my wonderful wife, Cynthia, a woman with too many virtues to list. She encouraged me to pursue apologetics at a very stressful time in my life and pointed my energies and curiosity in the right direction at a crucial time, as she so often does.

I thank God for her daily.

FOREWORD
BY RAVI ZACHARIAS

Having spoken across the globe for over four decades, I am consistently met with a set of similar questions, whether from business leaders in Chennai or students in Canada. One of the questions I am often asked is, "How can I believe the Bible is true?"

I am not surprised by this repeated refrain; there is no book in history that has been so studied, and sadly, so maligned, as the Holy Bible. Countless people through the decades have staked their very lives upon it. Others with equal fervor have sought to expel it.

Is the Bible mere fantasy, or is it fantastically true? Is there truth for every human being within its pages—the very Word of God to us—or only for a few? Supremely, its message stands or falls upon its authenticity.

These are the questions that Dan Buttafuoco addresses so capably in the work you hold in your hands. As he observes, "The Bible is a document we can use to examine whether the claims made in regard to our souls are true. If these claims are provably false, we need not worry about this subject at all. If they are true, we need to pay careful attention to what the Bible says."

I have known Dan for almost two decades. Although his role as a trial lawyer often brings its share of critics, he brims with insight, passion (he is Italian after all!), and a deep love for Christ and the Scriptures. In his professional life, he takes on some of the worthiest causes in need of defense. In this book to which his life is committed, he brings the best of his arguments and his keen mind as a lawyer to investigate the Bible. Whether you are a skeptic or a believer, I know you will find this to be an invaluable resource.

Ravi Zacharias, Best Selling
Author and Speaker

TABLE OF CONTENTS

INTRODUCTION

"...it is appointed unto men once to die, but after this, the judgment."—Hebrews 9:27

"Christianity, if false, is of no importance, and if true, of infinite importance. The only thing it cannot be is moderately important." C.S. Lewis

What if I told you that there was a book which compiled the themes, anecdotes, and turns of phrase on which you base your everyday life—would you want to know about it? How about a book that contained eyewitness testimony of some of the most legendary events and famous personalities in world history—would you be interested? What if I told you this same book was the very foundation for all of Western Civilization, containing the very principles and precepts upon which democracy and human rights were founded—would you want to read it?

You've probably caught on that I'm talking about the most well-known collection of books ever compiled: the

Bible—by far, the most important piece of writing ever published. The book you're holding now will attempt to explain why.

THE ISSUE

Christianity is a religion based on the information contained in the Bible. This means that over two billion people worldwide base their faith on a written document that is over 2,000 years old. That fact alone is amazing.

I am of Italian decent. In the Italian language there is a saying that goes: "Non è vero ma ci credo." Literally, this means "It's not true, but I believe it." Now, this might be an amusing insight on how some Italians view the world, but it's a totally unworkable and foolish way to live. Why would anyone want to believe something if it isn't true? I suppose that it might make some of us feel better to believe what we want to believe; but in reality, the only rational reason to believe something is because it's true.

> **Why would anyone want to believe something if it isn't true?**

Christianity is a religion that claims to speak the truth on some pretty heavy subjects. Specifically, Christians believe that one day, each of us will have to give an account to God for how we've lived our lives, that we will be judged for infractions of God's perfect and just laws. According to these teachings, our souls will spend eternity in heaven or hell based on how the Creator of the universe judges His creation: humans.

Christianity teaches that we are already on the losing side of this judgment. Due to our sinful nature, we can't possibly be good enough to merit eternal life based on our own ability to keep the perfect laws of God. Each of us has fallen short in some way in keeping these laws perfectly. This creates an obvious problem that affects all of humanity.

But Christianity also offers Good News. The good news is that God provided a way for us to be saved from being found guilty at His judgement. To save us, God paid the penalty for our sins by being born as a human being, remaining sinless, and dying in our place to satisfy His perfect justice. To save us from the consequences of our own actions, God placed the penalty for our sins upon Himself, allowing us to avoid the consequences of our guilt.

WHY IS THE BIBLE IMPORTANT?

The Bible is not just a collection of stories; it's also a historical document. We can use its depiction of history to examine whether the claims made in regard to our souls are true. If those claims are provably false, we need not worry about this subject at all. If they are true, we need to pay careful attention to what the Bible says.

In other words, if the Bible is not true, then it's of zero importance. But, if the Bible is true, then it's of monumental importance. The Bible, as set forth in the New Testament, is the foundation of Christianity. To paraphrase what C.S. Lewis said, "the only thing [the Bible] cannot be is moderately important."

The Bible consists of two main sections, the Old Testament (what Jews would call "the Tanakh") and the New Testament. The Christian faith utilizes both sections, but focuses primarily on the events and teachings contained in the New Testament.

> **The Bible is not just a collection of stories; it's also a historical document.**

Throughout this book, when the term "Bible" is used, I'll be referring primarily to the 27 writings or "books" that make up the New Testament. There are several reasons for this. First, the New Testament's importance to Christianity is such that, to prove the truth of the New Testament would be to prove the truth of Christianity. The second is a matter of simplification. This book would have to be much larger if it attempted to address the veracity of the Old Testament as well, as that discussion is more complex. Finally, the New Testament is so closely related to the Old Testament in terms of laws, cultures, customs, geography, and principles, that to prove the New Testament will also give strong credence to the Old Testament, which in turn, provides the requisite context and background for the New Testament.

The case for the Old Testament's veracity is slightly different and harder to make than the New Testament's, primarily because of the extreme age of the Old Testament and the amount of time that has passed since it was first written. Compared to the Old Testament, the New Testament is relatively, well, new.

The New Testament is close to 2,000 years old, while the Old Testament's age may be close to double that number. But, while I've decided to focus on the veracity of the New Testament, there are still several things that can be said pointing to the veracity of the Old Testament. For one thing, Jesus consistently verified the entirety of the Old Testament when he said "[t]he Scripture cannot be broken" (see John 10:35 and many other times where Jesus quoted or upheld the Old Testament as the very Word of God).

To a Jewish person like Jesus, the Bible or "Scripture" consisted of the Old Testament, also known as "The Tanakh." The Tanakh is foundational to the New Testament and is also considered Scripture by Christians. Both Old and New Testaments are considered the Word of God by Christians everywhere.

The Old Testament supplies so many quotes and references for the New Testament that it is clear that a venerated, compiled text of some sort had been around for a long time before the events of the New Testament occurred. You cannot truly understand the story of the New Testament without at least knowing something about the Old Testament. In this way, they are intertwined.

The Old Testament was taken for granted as a historical account by the Jewish people in the first century. This is clear to us in other historical accounts, not just the New Testament. Many of the same arguments about corroboration which are made concerning the New Testament apply to the Old Testament as well. The extreme age of the Old Testament makes it harder to corroborate the text with other sources due to the passage of time, the difficulty in finding artifacts, and the difficulty of preserving ancient texts for extended millennia.

The New Testament is the main source text for Christians, the believers and followers of Jesus Christ. It is where the Christian gains insight to the words of Jesus and the acts of the early Church. This is where Christian faith and practice are clearly spelled out. While the Christian Bible also contains the Old Testament, that ancient text is mainly there for the history it contains of God in dealing with mankind, primarily the Jewish people, and to demonstrate the character of God in the context of history. It provides the context for the New Testament events and sets the stage for the appearance of Jesus who was the fulfillment of the multiple specific prophecies that had been written down over the past centuries in the Old Testament.

This book is going to make the case for why the New Testament is of "infinite importance" to the world and why it is accurate and worthy of belief. It has veracity.

SO, WHAT IS THE BIBLE?

The Bible is a book concerned primarily with man's relationship with God. It is, among other things, a historical story about humans becoming separated from God (the Creator) because of our sinfulness and rebellion. Since it concludes with God's rescue of His people from their own sinfulness and the restoration of all things to Himself, it's also a story with a happy ending.

> The Bible is not a single work by a single author (unless one were to call God, Himself, the author)

The Bible is not a single work by a single author (unless one were to call God, Himself, the author). It's a collection of ancient writings, written over a period of 1,500 years, by approximately 40 different authors. These writings are compiled in a book we now call "the Bible." The Bible consists of 66 "books" in total, divided into two large sections: the Old Testament and the New Testament.

The word "Bible" comes from the Greek word "byblos," which simply means "book." The earliest Christians were, for the most part, of Jewish heritage. As such, they considered Jesus to be the continuation and fulfillment of the Old Testament (the first section). The second large section is called the New Testament. The writings in the New Testament comprise the essentials of the Christian faith, beginning with the genealogy and life of Jesus. There are 39 books in the Old Testament and 27 books in the New Testament. Christians believe that these 66 books form the sum total of God's revelation to mankind about Himself, the state of man, and God's plan for redemption.

The New Testament tells the story of Jesus of Nazareth, also called Jesus, the Christ or Jesus, the Messiah. Messiah is Hebrew and Christ is Greek for "Anointed One." In the Bible, Jesus is shown to be the fulfillment of all of the prophecies that are written in the Old Testament about the one who would come to rescue mankind from its plight of separation from God due to sin. These prophecies are numerous, and many are highly specific. This alone is remarkable. That any single person could fulfill over 300 separate prophecies is statistically amazing.

The New Testament is classified into four distinct parts. The first consists of four books called "the Gospels" (Matthew, Mark, Luke, and John). The word gospel means "good news." These books record the words and actions of Jesus as well as His death, burial, and resurrection. The story is told four different times by four different authors. At the end of each unique account, Jesus is shown to be the triumphant conqueror over the grave and over evil. The good news here is God's redemption plan taking place in the person and life of Jesus Christ. That is the central point of the New Testament and the culmination of the entire Bible.

The four Gospel authors are sometimes called the "Four Witnesses." They differ in some of their details because they each tell the story of Jesus from a different vantage point. Most biblical scholars have concluded that the Gospel of Mark was essentially written by Peter, a disciple of Jesus. Scholars believe that Mark acted as Peter's "amanuensis" (i.e. secretary) and was taking dictation from Peter (a relatively uneducated fisherman). So, Matthew, Mark (Peter), and John are all firsthand eyewitness accounts of the life of Jesus. They were his friends, his traveling companions, and his disciples. They were the ones chosen to transmit the story of Jesus as historical fact down through the eons of time.

Luke, a Greek physician, was not an actual eyewitness to Jesus' ministry, but did write a gospel account. Luke's gospel is also an eyewitness account, even though Luke was not, himself, an eyewitness. Acting as an investigative reporter, Luke interviewed various witnesses and compiled a book of their testimonies to show the world what Jesus did and what Jesus said. We know this to be true because of the introduction to his book:

> "Many have undertaken to draw up an account of the things that have been fulfilled among us, just as they were handed down to us by those who from the first were eyewitnesses and servants of the word. With this in mind, since I myself have carefully investigated everything from the beginning, I too decided to write an orderly account for you, most excellent Theophilus, so that you may know the certainty of the things you have been taught."[1]

Luke records actual historical facts and his account is a transcript of eyewitness accounts.

The second part of the New Testament is the standalone Book of Acts. Also written by Luke, it is another historical account of the exploits and the persecution of the early Church. The word church is a translation of the Greek word *ecclesia* and means simply the "called-out ones." The followers of Jesus, a small band of people, grew to a large, worldwide movement as the news of Jesus' life and resurrection spread throughout the world. In Luke's second volume, he is an actual eyewitness to the "acts" of the Apostles and the early Church as they followed the teachings of Jesus.

The word *Christian* was originally a derogatory term. It was used as an insult to label the earliest believers in Ephesus (modern-day Turkey). It literally meant "little Christ." That definition has changed somewhat over the centuries to mean "follower of Christ," and to signify the adherents of an entirely new religion. The key word here is "follower."

To be a Christian, one must be an actual follower of Jesus Christ. Your birth, religion, nationality, and parents have only a small part to play here. This truth may make some people uncomfortable, but it's entirely possible for someone to be raised in a Christian home in a Christian country, educated in a Christian school, and not be a follower of Christ.

The word *Christian* was originally a derogatory term.

To be a follower of Jesus requires us to know some things about Him. We cannot follow someone we know nothing or little about. We can't copy the leader if we don't know the leader. The early Church's response to the brief, miraculous life of Jesus is recorded in the Book of Acts. The early Church's attempt to "follow" Christ is recorded there.

The third part of the New Testament is made up of the "Epistles," which means "letters." These are actual letters written by the Apostles (or people very close to them) to the early Church about how to be a follower of Jesus Christ. The Epistles contain words of wisdom and instruction for all believers in Jesus, providing a practical guide to Christian living and faith. Again, to "follow" Christ is the goal.

The last part of the New Testament is a single book called "The Revelation." It records the final revealing and return of Jesus Christ in the future. It's a book of prophetic writing, detailing how God will redeem and judge the world. Some of that book has already been fulfilled. More is yet to come.

It's obvious that everyday believers need to understand why the Bible is considered to be the supernatural, divine Word of God. If it is the Word of God, as it claims to be, then we ignore its warnings at our own peril. If we decide to heed its warnings, then it must be carefully studied, interpreted, and obeyed as closely as possible. This is the mandate of Scripture. Despite its historical content, scripture doesn't exist solely to inform us about history. It's God's Word to us, His instructions on how to avoid eternal punishment. And once we are saved from that terrible fate, Scripture provides us with clear directions for living a righteous life, including practical advice and wisdom for successful living, now and for eternity.

Whether or not one is a Christian, one should have some basic understanding of the Bible and its claims.

The Bible is foundational to almost every enterprise in the entire world. It's truly that important from a historical point of view. What I want to emphasize is how critical the Bible is in terms of its impact on the world and upon humanity. This is true about the Bible whether you're a Christian or not. So, no matter how you regard it, the Bible is a "must read" book.

Part of what I engage in is Christian "apologetics." Apologetics is the art and science of persuasion.[2] Christianity is really only spread by persuasion. It claims to be the truth. It is that which comports with reality about God, man, and our plight. The Bible is unashamed in making these claims.

All religions claim to be "The Truth," which means, they cannot all be true since they all contradict each other. The issue, then, is to seek out and discover which is the right teaching about God, and which teachings are wrong.

This short book explains why Christians believe the Bible is the truth, why we believe that it is the literal and actual Word of God. I hope that this book will put the Bible into perspective for you and cause you to consider the words on its pages with grave seriousness.

EXHIBIT A

THE BIBLE HAS
TRANSFORMED
THE WORLD

"In the beginning was the Word, and the Word was with God, and the Word was God."

—John 1:1

The Bible has a destination in mind. It's a story with a purpose—a roadmap. This roadmap is firmly planted in actual events, giving credence to the fact that it leads to an actual, real-life, non-mythological destination. The destination I speak of is not a place—it's a person.

The Bible's main purpose is to introduce you to a real person who exists in real life. That person is none other than God, Himself. That person made Himself available to us to know, to love (or to hate), to accept (or to reject), to live for (or to ignore).

> **The Bible has a destination in mind. It's a story with a purpose–a roadmap.**

He is totally good, yet controversial, funny, supremely intelligent, all-powerful, awesomely majestic, incredibly beautiful, and (amazingly) willing to have a personal relationship with us. His name is Jesus and He is, and was, and ever will be, God in human form. He is the very God who, for His own reasons and out of His love for us, came to Earth at an appointed place and time so that He might present Himself to us in a way that we might get to know Him.

DIVERSITY

The 66 books of the Bible were written by approximately 40 separate authors from various walks of life. These authors were prophets, priests, kings, princes, nobility, lawyers, judges, at least one physician, professional scribes, government leaders, intellectuals, shepherds, farmers, peasants, fishermen, and prisoners. These authors all had one thing in common: their writing was recognized early on as having a special quality, the quality of someone who

1. had a close encounter with God
2. had something to say about God or His people
3. was in a position to have access to the truth about God.

If you took 40 people today and put them into a room and asked each of them to write a different section of the same book, almost instantly you'd run into all kinds of problems. First of all, you'd never get them to agree on anything. Their writings would contradict each other on practically every page. They would have different opinions on the story's ending and argue over how to describe the characters. If you asked them to write about God, it would be even worse.

But, miraculously, although 40 different authors wrote it over a span of 1,500 years (from approximately 1400 BC to 100 AD) the Bible agrees with itself. The different vantage points of the various authors come together in a seamless whole, like a tapestry, making a beautiful portrait of God in His dialogues with people. This is why the Bible is often discussed as a single "book" even though it is a compilation of 66 separate writings.

NEW IDEAS

The Bible contains ideas that have literally shaped the Western world. Even if you're not a believer, if you claim to be somewhat intelligent, you really can't claim to have a basic understanding of Western civilization if you don't understand the Bible. It's truly that important and foundational to civilization and society. This is especially true of the New Testament.

> The Bible contains ideas that have literally shaped the Western world.

As an example, many expressions that we use in everyday language come from the Bible. This demonstrates how ingrained the Bible is into our everyday customs and our culture.

Expressions include: "Knocked off his high horse," "fight the good fight," "fly in the ointment," "drop in the bucket," "daily bread," "a labor of love," "thorn in the flesh," "wolf in sheep's clothing," "my brother's keeper," "an eye for an eye," "turn the other cheek," "old as the hills," "white as snow," "the skin of your teeth," "eat, drink, and be merry," and "cross to bear."

All of these phrases have Biblical origins.

When President Abraham Lincoln famously said, "A house divided against itself cannot stand," he could very easily have added, "By the way, I'm borrowing this from Jesus!" The people in that setting knew he was quoting the words of Jesus, as recorded in the Bible. This is just another example of the importance of the Bible for the ideas and the thoughts that it conveys, whether you believe it's a sacred text or not. It's deeply ingrained into Western culture and thought. In recent years, it has started to shape the Far East, as well.

The Lord's Prayer, recorded in the Book of Matthew, Chapter 6, is probably the most famous prayer recorded in the Western world. If you do a Google search and simply type the word "our," you'll see it come up immediately. Just three letters from a common word brings the entire prayer immediately to your computer screen! That's how often people look for this prayer.

The prayer, as recorded in Matthew, reads as follows:

"Our Father in heaven, hallowed be your name,
your kingdom come, your will be done,
on earth as it is in heaven.
Give us today our daily bread. And forgive us our debts,
as we also have forgiven our debtors.
And lead us not into temptation,
but deliver us from the evil one."[1]

This prayer was revolutionary. It was highly unusual at the time Jesus first prayed these words to refer to God as "our Father."[2] To address God, the Creator of all things, in this way was considered far too intimate, much too familiar. Jesus changed all of that with this simple prayer. We take for granted the concept of "God, the Father" but it's first recorded in the Bible. That alone is groundbreaking. Jesus had a unique relationship with God and he taught that we all can have a similar relationship with Him.

THE BIBLE PREACHES NON-VIOLENCE

Unlike other religious texts, the New Testament does not encourage anyone to commit violence. Under no interpretation of the New Testament can anyone find a single justification for causing harm to another human being, or to intentionally do them damage. According to the New Testament, we are not even to speak badly about others (Colossians 3:8; James 4:11; 1 Timothy 5:13)!

In the New Testament, we are taught to absorb hurts and walk away from conflict. Christians are not to retaliate against people who are against us. The command of Jesus is to "do unto others as you would have them do unto you" (Luke 6:31). We are not to treat others as they treat us, but as we would want them to treat us. That's a big difference. The standard of how we treat others is how we would like to be treated. That's amazing in its simplicity and beauty. Even when insulted or attacked, we are never to respond with violence.

Instead, when someone strikes us on one cheek, Jesus teaches us to "turn the other cheek" (Matthew 5:38–40). Jesus, Himself, modeled this behavior when He absorbed the taunts, insults, beatings, and torture of his accusers without so much as offering a word in his defense. How different this is from other so-called "holy" prophets who were utterly selfish in their pursuits and who wreaked vengeance on their adversaries for the slightest insults "in the name of God."

The Apostle Paul tells us in Romans, "If it is possible, far as it depends on you, live at peace with everyone" (Romans 12:18). In this day of suicide bombers and religious lunatics blowing up innocent children in the name of religion, it's comforting to know that the Bible, as set forth in the New Testament scriptures, not only does not encourage violence, but absolutely commands the opposite. It preaches peace on earth and goodwill to men (Luke 2:14).

So, let's not pretend that "all religions are equal." Clearly, they are not. Other religious scriptures actually encourage violence and warfare. While it's not this book's purpose to debate this issue, it's not a hard case to prove, in spite of those who wish to whitewash the truth and pretend that such admonitions in their scriptures to attack and fight "unbelievers" are merely "spiritual." History proves this beyond any doubt. The Old Testament contains references to warfare and killing, but nowhere in the New Testament is this condoned. No one can make the case that the New Testament teaches violence or retaliation.

This is not an indictment against the concept of self-defense or, on a greater scale, what can be termed a "just war," one in which a people are called to protect themselves from an unjust attack or the threat of extinction. That is necessary in the face of real evil. We need self-defense at times, individually and as a nation. But those situations are rare.

Violence, killing, and the hurting of others simply is not a Christian concept. The Bible in the New Testament is a peace-loving book devoid of violence by Christians. In fact, the only recorded violence in the New Testament is against Christians who suffer silently and without retaliation. What a tremendous difference that is from other religions. Only the woefully uninformed or the willfully dishonest could argue otherwise.

LANGUAGE, CULTURE, AND HISTORY

The Bible was instrumental in forming the English language, one of the major languages of the world.

William Tyndale was one of the most important and influential people to have ever lived.[3] He was a brilliant linguist, translator, and theologian.[4] He is important even from a secular perspective in terms of the English language and the words he invented. He created many of the words we use today on a regular basis, including the word "beautiful." Tyndale translated the Bible into English almost singlehandedly. It was his life's work. We would not have the English language were it not for William Tyndale, and we wouldn't have William Tyndale without the Bible. The overwhelming majority of his work went into developing the King James Bible. He

> The Bible was instrumental in forming the English language, one of the major languages of the world.

is considered by many to be the "architect of the English language."[5]

The Bible has transformed the world because of the history it records, including the history of the ancient world. It has transformed the world because of language, it has transformed the world because of ideas, and it has transformed the world because of culture. The Exodus, the crucifixion of Jesus, the Resurrection, and the formation of the early Church all are monumental facts of history described in detail in the Bible. These historical accounts are memorialized in holidays that billions of people celebrate to this very day. They are also the subject of countless books and motion pictures.

Christians and Jews consult the history of the Bible to try to understand God's actions as they are demonstrated through real historical events. In the Bible, we have examples of how God interacts with mankind. This gives us insight into His character. We want to know Who God is and what He wants, what He likes and what He dislikes.

The Bible is also foundational to many great enterprises. There are Christian churches, hospitals, orphanages, disaster response teams, and ministries that feed and clothe people, all of which have their foundation in the Bible. How many hospitals do you know that have "St. Mary," or "St. Joseph," or the word "Lutheran" in front of their names? The list is vast.

In terms of transforming the world, even in architecture and art, the Bible has impacted our lives and cultures in a tremendous way. For example, there would not be massive cathedrals without the Bible. Many museums and libraries would not exist. Europe would look entirely different if the Bible had never existed. Some of these buildings took hundreds of years to construct. The motivation for these great works was the facts contained in the Bible.

Much of the world's art is based on the Bible. Most Renaissance pieces have biblical influences. In fact, Renaissance art, even good Renaissance art, is surprisingly cheap because there's so much of it. You can buy a good quality Renaissance painting for roughly ten thousand dollars. Shocking, right? The artists are long dead, so you would normally expect the value to be much higher. But, without the Bible, the Renaissance might never have even happened!

How about books that were written about the Bible? If you stacked all the books written and published about the Bible on top of each other, they would reach to the moon. Artwork, books, songs, and music written about the Bible, when totaled together, constitute a massive amount of material. Even secular books of great literature have strong Christian themes. Without the Bible, you wouldn't have the works of Shakespeare, Dostoevsky, Tolstoy, Dante, Goethe, Augustine, and many others too numerous to list. Shakespeare, alone, quoted from the Geneva Bible over 5,000 times.[6]

We see that the Bible is foundational in transforming the world through language and culture. How about milestones in communications? We immediately think about the Gutenberg Bible—the first book ever printed![7] Johannes Gutenberg invented the movable type printing press in 1455, on which he printed the Bible.[8] That began the mass production of books and is arguably the starting point of the Renaissance. It began the widespread dissemination of knowledge and learning.

So, it's fitting, then, that the first book ever printed was the Bible. This is tremendously important in terms of communications. The printing press with moveable type transformed the world and the scholarly community, and it all started with the Bible being printed. The Bible is the most published book in history. Since the New Testament was able to be mass-produced, the Bible has been the top bestseller year after year. That alone is amazing. Every year it beats every other book printed in terms of production and distribution. An author gets excited if their book is on the bestseller list for several weeks. The Bible is the bestseller every year! (There is the exception of one year in the 1960s when it was surpassed by the sayings of Mao Zedong, the Chinese Communist dictator, which was forced into print not by popular demand but by his decree, so that really shouldn't count.)[9] The demand for the Bible is constant and robust.

The Bible has been translated into every known language, including Braille, and is constantly being translated into newly-discovered languages. If anthropologists go into the mountains of Peru or in a remote Amazon area, they'll sometimes discover a group of people that speaks an unknown language. Almost immediately, Bible societies get to work on translating the Bible into their language. Biblical societies exist for this very purpose.

Now, the Bible is having a massive impact on Eastern civilization. By some estimates, approximately 30,000 people per day in China are coming to a belief in the Bible and faith in Christ.[10] The bottom line is this: over TWO BILLION people call themselves Christians today. That's just remarkable.

The existence of the Church itself, even in its current form with many sects and denominations of Christianity, is a testimony to the life of Jesus, the actions of the first-century Church, and the events that followed. The Bible records the mission and challenges of the early Church, the first disciples of Jesus. Christianity is a movement that started with a band of uneducated and disparate followers that were hiding out, terrified that they were going to be the next people executed by crucifixion, and yet they literally, as the Bible says, "turned the world upside down."[11] Take the Bible out of the world and the world looks very different. You cannot comprehend the world without some knowledge of the Bible.

MORALS DO NOT JUST "HAPPEN"

Most of human morality is based on the Bible. Whether you realize it or not, most of what you believe to be right and wrong is based on the Bible.

> Take the Bible out of the world and the world looks very different.

Confucius taught to "do unto others as they do unto you." This is essentially what most people feel inclined to do. It's easy to treat others with kindness if they've treated you kindly. It also implies that you can treat people harshly if they treat you harshly. But this is nothing more than human nature.

Jesus, as recorded in the Bible, substantially raised this bar. He taught us to treat people as we would want to be treated, not as they actually treat us. If this rule were universally followed, there would literally be no wars, no murders, no rapes, and no fights.

The Bible, then, teaches a high standard of morality. It records rules, given by God, for how people are to live successfully and happily. Jesus said, "He who hears these words of Mine and does them is like a wise man who built his house on the rock."[12]

More than any other book, the Bible records a higher form of morality in terms of dealing with our fellow human beings. Jesus taught what is now known as the "Golden Rule," which says to "do unto others as you would have them do unto you."[13]

It is truly a "golden rule." This principle is widely recognized as the most significant and noble principle ever taught by all religious leaders, and we have the Bible to thank for it.

> The man of the world repays good for good
>   and evil for evil.
> The man of evil repays evil for good.
> The man of God repays good for evil.
>   —author unknown

Now, just because the Bible teaches a high morality doesn't mean that Christians always follow it. Critics of Christianity like to argue that Christians commit bad acts or do "bad things." Unfortunately, this is absolutely true. Christians don't always behave well. But, the problem isn't the Bible or the teachings of Jesus. When a Christian does "bad things," it's because he or she is not following the teachings of Christ. When members of other religions commit murder, rape, and other "bad things" in some cases, they're actually following their religious teachings. When Christians commit evil, they are violating the commands of the New Testament. That's a huge difference. The New Testament forbids treating people badly. It preaches kindness, sacrifice, and mercy.

Even the leaders of the Church have behaved badly. For example, in the late Middle Ages, the organized church was against having the Bible in the common tongue of the people and demanded that the Bible be printed only in Latin.[14] It was especially true that Church authorities didn't want the Bible to be available in English. As a result, any Bible prepared in English prior to 1539 was a "forbidden book."[15] The Church authorities behaved terribly in forbidding the Bible to be read by people and punishing them for the "crime" of owning a copy of the Bible in English. People were even burned at the stake for printing the Bible in English, or even having a Bible in English.

During the Renaissance, the Popes were known for their evil behavior, violence, and depravity. In a section of her book, entitled *The Renaissance Popes Provoke the Protestant Secession*, Barbara W. Tuchman chronicles the abuses of Church leadership at the highest levels. Using historical sources, she paints a picture of a papacy that was anything but "Christian." If these Popes followed Christ even for a moment, it was purely by accident. In her book, *The March of Folly*, Tuchman quotes Giovanni de' Medici as saying, "Flee, we are in the hands of a wolf," upon the elevation of Rodrigo Borgia to the papacy.[16]

In Chapter 3 entitled "Depravity: Alexander VI, 1492-1503," she writes in detail of the evils of Pope Alexander VI (Rodrigo Borgia), including murder, greed, warfare, open adultery, lying, and extortion (only a partial list). His life would have made a stripper blush. Even Roman Catholic sources refer to him as "criminal, dissolute and corrupt."[17] Unfortunately, his behavior was not unique.

The fact that we can criticize the lives, behavior, and character of even religious leaders points to the Bible as the objective moral standard by which we can legitimately measure someone claiming to be a Christian, a follower of Christ. Clearly, even some Popes were not truly Christian! They did not follow the New Testament or the commands of Jesus, and that is what defines a Christian.

THE BIBLE BECOMES WIDELY AVAILABLE TO THE PUBLIC

It's no coincidence that the Renaissance occurs at the same time that the Bible is made available to the public at-large.

In the first 400–500 years of Christianity, the Bible was widely available in manuscript form to people in the churches. In the early churches, it was read aloud. After the Fall of Rome, civilization regressed as barbarians and illiterate tribes invaded and conquered one another. Europe was steeped in turmoil.

For the period sometimes referred to as "The Dark Ages," from approximately 500 A.D. to 1000 A.D., people were too busy trying to survive to concern themselves with learning. During this time, literacy among the populace declined. As a result, only the most educated people had access to a Bible. This consisted, primarily, of "religious" people who were Church officials or members of monasteries or other religious orders. The average person only had access to the teachings of the Bible indirectly through the sermons and the artwork they

> **Some did a decent job and others didn't do so well. Nothing, however, could substitute for reading the Scriptures for oneself.**

experienced in Church buildings. This is why most Churches from that time period were highly decorated with biblical scenes. The goal was to communicate the message and stories of the Bible to mostly illiterate people.

Without being able to read the Bible for themselves, the general public was at the mercy of the clergy for the information and teachings of Christ. Some did a decent job and others didn't do so well. Nothing, however, could substitute for reading the Scriptures for oneself.

What was needed was a Bible available for all to read. Church authorities were ambivalent about this, at best; and at worst, hostile to the idea. The reason for this was that it was politically dangerous for the organized church to allow the Bible into the hands of the common people. After all, if they could read it for themselves, they would be informed and empowered to criticize the Church or the nobility for how far they had strayed from the teachings of Jesus!

Erasmus of Rotterdam was the first to print the Bible in Greek in 1516.[18] He was careful to do this in a way that avoided angering Pope Leo X. He walked a fine line between antagonizing the church authorities and getting the Bible into the hands of the masses. His was an important first step.

Once the Greek Bible of 1516 was printed, it was only a matter of time before someone translated the Bible into English or some other country's natural language. Martin Luther translated the Bible into German in 1522 and William Tyndale translated the Bible into English in 1525. Both Bibles were illegal and forbidden books, swiftly banned by the Church. In fact, all of the early translations of the Bible into English were illegal until 1539, when the first English Bible was printed with the permission of King Henry VIII. The Pope was still against this idea, but since Henry VIII had separated the Church of England from the Roman Catholic Church, he simply didn't care.

In 1611, the King James Bible was printed as an authorized English translation with permission from King

James I of England (VI of Scotland). The King James Version was based primarily on a handful of medieval manuscripts.[19] The New Testament in English from the King James Version was based on the "Textus Receptus" or "received text." This was the third edition of a printer named Stephanas who produced such a book in 1550 based on Erasmus' 1516 New Testament. So, it can be fairly said that the King James Version of the New Testament was based on seven or eight late manuscripts. That's not much in the way of original writings. Even so, subsequent manuscript discoveries show it was highly accurate. We have more letters and manuscripts available today, making contemporary Bibles even more accurate.

In fairness to the organized Church, some sincere scholars and church leaders of those days believed that the Bible could not be understood by the average person, and that was a pretty fair assessment since the average person of the Middle Ages was unable to read. The Church authorities were afraid that evil and ignorant people would twist the Scripture to fit their own illegitimate ends and try to use it as a means of control over people's minds and hearts. History shows us that this fear was not unfounded.

Once the Bible became available to the masses it opened up its pages for all types of people, some of whom had bad intentions. But this actually proves the power of the Bible. The Bible was and still is considered so authoritative that people are able to use it to create a cult or lead people astray. The organized church was rightly concerned about this. The Church was afraid of the power of the Bible in the hands of the average person.

The fact that the Bible can be misused by evil people is not a basis to keep the Word of God from people. It only means that we should try even harder to ascertain its true meaning. The best way to correct a poor interpretation of the Bible is by careful study to understand the correct interpretation. People who misuse the Bible typically take a single verse out of context and "spin" it to mean what they want it to say. But the Bible is very clear on the main points it wants to convey. When something is not clear, one just needs to keep reading until the point is clarified by additional passages. Even though people try to "spin" the Bible for their own ends, these errors are exposed when the context is carefully examined. The main tenets of the Bible are repeated so often and in so many places that they are impossible to miss.

> **The fact that the Bible can be misused by evil people is not a basis to keep the Word of God from people.**

As an example of this, prior to the Civil War, slave owners (who were mostly Southern American Protestants) attempted to use the Bible to justify slavery. They cited passages that mentioned slavery without condemning it. What they failed to admit, due to their own special interests, was that the Bible only mentions slavery in passing as a fact of life that existed in the ancient world. The Bible neither condoned nor forbade slavery ("slavery" as it existed during ancient times was a very different practice than what existed in America).[20]

That's because the Bible is concerned with an even larger issue: the condition of our own slavery to our own selfish desires in the context of a Creator God who wants us perfect, good, and right. Our slavery to ourselves is the very issue Jesus came to address. Everything else in the Bible is secondary. The Bible deals with the issue of human nature and our propensity to gravitate towards selfishness to the harm of ourselves and others. It is every man's slavery to his own sin that is at the heart of the message of the Bible.

THE BIBLE TELLS THE TRUTH ABOUT GOD

The power of the Bible to change the world rests on the fact that the Bible tells the truth about God and mankind's relation to him. The Bible reveals the heart of man and answers the big questions of life: Who am I? Where did I come from? What is my purpose? What will happen when I die? The Bible puts life in context with eternity. It's because the Bible tells the truth about the important issues of life that it transforms people, relationships, cultures, and governments. Jesus knew this. Jesus was very concerned with this concept of truth. Jesus knew that truth was found in Scripture, the very words of God. He, like most Jews of his time, studied the Bible.

Jesus knew the Bible better than we can even imagine. Most Christians have no idea how intimately familiar Jesus was with Scripture. There is a story in the Gospel of Luke that makes this point, but you have to know a little more information to really appreciate it:

"And He [Jesus] came to Nazareth, where He had been brought up; and as was His custom, He entered the synagogue on the Sabbath, and stood up to read. And the book of the prophet Isaiah was handed to Him. And He opened the book and found the place where it was written, 'The Spirit of the Lord is upon me, because He anointed me to preach the gospel to the poor. He has sent me to proclaim release to the captives, and recovery of sight to the blind, to set free those who are oppressed, to proclaim the favorable year of the Lord.' And He closed the book, gave it back to the attendant and sat down; and the eyes of all in the synagogue were fixed on Him."[21]

Most people miss exactly what a remarkable feat Jesus performed here in front of the entire congregation. We live in a day where preachers preach from laptops and iPads. These things have "search" features. What

Jesus was reading here was a scroll. A scroll was a very primitive form of "book" that was far more difficult to use.

What's really amazing is how these scrolls were made. They consisted of many animal skins (typically sheepskins) sewn together to form a big heavy scroll that has long handles at both ends, so that as one side is unrolled the other one can be rolled to pick up the slack. They were huge, clumsy objects and quite heavy. If the Isaiah scroll were completely unrolled, it would be something approximating 25 feet long (the Torah unrolled is about 120 feet long!).

They were all written by hand (these things were made way before printing existed) and were only written on one side of the skin surface. The Romans improved on this design by inventing what is known as the codex, a form of the modern book with which we are familiar today (having rectangular pages written on both

Scrolls were big and clumsy compared to a codex, and they were at least twice as large as they needed to be.

sides between two covers). The advantage of the codex was that it allowed writing to be placed on both sides of the skins so that one could turn a page and see the opposite side of the skin.

This was a big improvement in a day when materials were scarce because it doubled the size of the writing surface. Scrolls were big and clumsy compared to a codex, and they were at least twice as large as they needed to be. Add to that the wooden spool handles at either end and scrolls were cumbersome objects that were difficult to use and to read, especially in public when everyone was watching. This is exactly what Jesus did in this passage of Scripture quoted above. He was handed the scroll and had to search for the passage of Scripture that He wanted to read in public to make his point. Now this is not an easy task unless you're very familiar with the Bible, and in particular, the Book of Isaiah; a very large book, one of longest in the Bible. This was no laptop. This was not even a codex!

But, it gets even more complicated. The Hebrew written on the Isaiah scroll is not written with any punctuation or even spaces between the words. This means that the text in this big, heavy scroll is literally one long writing without spaces, sort of like one single gigantic word that runs the entire length of the scroll (let me remind you, the scroll is nearly ten yards long). There are no spaces, no paragraphs, and no punctuation— and in ancient Hebrew, there were no vowels! The reader had to know where to put the vowels! This means that any person reading this object would need an amazing grasp of the Hebrew written language. Furthermore, to get up in public and find the exact verse you wanted to read, while people in the congregation were looking at you and watching expectantly, was quite a feat! This indicates that Jesus knew the Book of Isaiah (and I am certain the entire Bible) like nobody we can imagine. He was literally an expert in the entire text to be able to find that exact verse in such a confusing and cumbersome scroll in time to read it publicly. Wow!

If Jesus, who was the "Word made flesh,"[22] knew the Bible so intimately, isn't it just as important, if not more so, for us to know the Word of God? Not many years ago, all Christians believed this. Christians made it their duty to read, study, and even memorize parts of the Bible. Unfortunately, in the modern age, most people have largely ignored the Bible. This is a travesty. Is it any wonder that Christians don't know or understand their own faith? And, if they're not reading the Bible, it's not surprising to see Christians that don't act like Christ.

People often state that all religions basically accomplish the same thing. Coupled with the fact that there seems to be so much confusion and fighting between various religious groups, why not avoid the topic altogether and assign equal status to all religions everywhere in the hope that people can all "just get along?" Religious ideas, people say, should just be relegated to the private sphere and shouldn't be discussed or debated because this breeds strife. After all, since it's so hard (some say "impossible") to figure out who's right, why bother?

There is no doubt that this is an attractive approach to many people. It also takes the burden from people to do the "heavy lifting" associated with verifying the truth claims of various sects and religions, which requires hours of seeking, reading, and study of the vast amount of material both for and against a particular point. While the Internet has made this much easier, it's still a huge task. Simply put, people really don't want to bother taking part in the search for religious truth anymore. After all, it's much easier to spend hours looking at funny cat videos on social media.

The claims of the Bible, however, are too important to ignore.

TRUTH IS UNAVOIDABLE

The problem with truth is that it smacks you in the face when you least expect it. You may try to avoid it or deny it, but it doesn't go away. It shows up suddenly and mocks you if you're on the wrong side of it. It can't be deferred or "wished away." It is immutable.

Truth is important for its own sake even if it comes at a considerable price. I would rather try to discover the truth about God, the cosmos, humanity, life after death, judgment, sin, accountability, and the nature of reality than leave such important questions to chance. I want to know and understand these things while there is breath and life in me and I can make meaningful changes about how to live my life. "I'll find out when I die" is a risky strategy for your appointment with God—eternity is an awfully long time!

The sad fact is that most people don't even try. Coupled with the fact that there are many half-truths, downright ridiculous ideas, and even outright lies out there about God, it's a daunting task. The Bible is the clearest way to get a good idea about these topics since the people who wrote it had direct contact with God or someone close to Him.

> I've heard some ask, "But, isn't it true that in religion what is 'true' for you may not be 'true' for me, and vice versa?" In response, I would ask, "Is that even possible?

If there is one thing that marks truth, it is this: there is always a cost that goes along with finding it, revealing it, speaking it or ignoring it. Lies and flattery are meant to be palatable and always come with a motive. Truth, however, stands on its own and is always valuable for its own sake. Truth about God is especially important.

The Bible contains the truth that transformed the world. Once people grasp this truth, it ignites a passion within them to perform all kinds of feats. It is the truth of the Bible that gives it its power. Truth is powerful. Truth about God is nuclear. It's transformative.

I've heard some ask, "But, isn't it true that in religion what is 'true' for you may not be 'true' for me, and vice versa?" In response, I would ask, "Is that even possible? Is there such a thing as a private truth rather than objective truth? Doesn't the very word 'truth' imply that it's an objective statement of that which comports with reality?" No matter how much you may want to believe that the Cubs lost the 2016 World Series, no amount of wishful thinking would make this true. The claim that "there is no such thing as absolute truth" is really the tired and worn mantra of a postmodern generation that has given up on seeking, analyzing, and debating the respective merit of various ideologies. It has become a convenient cop out for the intellectually lazy.

By putting forth the disclaimer, "There is no such thing as absolute truth," people seek to avoid divisive controversy. While that might be a laudable goal, it's a position that makes no logical sense. Saying that there is no such thing as absolute truth is, itself, a claim of "absolute truth." The speaker is effectively saying, "It's absolutely true that nothing is absolutely true!" It's a ridiculous thing to say; and since it's clearly untrue, then the statement actually proves that something can be absolutely true. By attempting to deny it you actually affirm it! Absolute truth, therefore, must exist.

The quest, then, is to find the truth even if it means discarding our cherished beliefs once they are discovered to be patently false. Many people cannot, or will not, do this.

"Religion is the opium of the masses," said Karl Marx.[23] In this worldview, religion is something which gives people a "crutch" to get through the trials and tribulations of life, something that will help us "feel good," even if there is no reality behind it. If we believe it to be true, then it is "true for us" and then it works to give us comfort, hope, rules of moral conduct, and effective ways to relate to one another in a world of vicious competition for scarce resources. That is most people's view of "religion" or "religious ideas."

So, it should be no surprise that people see no need to defend one set of religious beliefs or "truth claims" over another equally effective but opposite set of "truth claims" by a different religion. If it works to help you or it makes you feel better, then who really cares what you believe? This, of course, all depends on your idea of what is the essential nature and function of religion. As I said above, if you believe that religion is essentially only man-made philosophical ideas that are only meant to work for you, then there's no reason to contend over whether those notions are objectively or absolutely true.

In this respect, and viewed solely from this vantage point, all religions are indeed the same. Essentially, all the religions of the world hold to similar beliefs and values: don't hurt people, don't take what doesn't belong to you (whether a man's wife or his cattle), don't kill, don't lie, honor your parents, etc. These values are found almost universally in most cultures and nations. The fact that there is such a remarkable consistency in all cultures across time and geography with respect to human cultural values points strongly to the existence of a certain absolute, objective moral truth. This suggests an objective moral "Law Giver" as a source for all these moral values. It cannot be by chance that every culture came up with these same values.

Sure, there are differences between cultures in terms of how these values are displayed and observed in various settings, but the essential core values are remarkably similar. Therefore, it's self-evident that (at least according to some) all religions are equal because they are all effective at accomplishing the same goals. Again, of course, that depends on your view of the essential nature of religion, "religious ideas," and moral values.

Suppose, for a moment, that religion is not man-made at all. Suppose that there really is a core of truth about God and that it is His values that these various religions reflect, to a greater or lesser degree. What if the reason all religions and cultures across time and space are so similar is that they are each an attempt to communicate these objective moral values (God's values) to their respective cultural groups? This is strong evidence, then, for the existence of God because, once you come to the conclusion that objective moral values exist, it's a short leap in logic to ask "Whose values? Where do they come from?"

Suppose further that the main purpose of religion is not only to tell us how we ought to relate to one another, but to tell us how to relate to the Creator (God), Himself? Is it not true, then, that it would be absolutely essential to know exactly what this Creator expects from us? It would do us utterly no good to invent our own rules or presume to manufacture our own "truth" in such a case since, it's obvious that what would really matter would be the Creator's values and wishes, not our own.

As a crude but workable example, if I were a foreigner in a strange country, I would need to pay my restaurant bill in the local currency. I might offer to pay in dollars. I might think that dollars are a "better" currency. I might view dollars as more reasonable to accept. I might understand dollars better. Regardless of my personal preferences, what would dictate an appropriate response on my part would be the objective reality of the financial requirements of that sovereign nation. My own preference of how to pay and in what currency would be meaningless. Similarly, when it comes to God, we ought to "render unto God, that which is God's,"[24] and not something else that we arbitrarily deem to be a suitable substitute. It's nothing but arrogance to think that we can make our own rules about what's important to God.

The issue of who sets the rules comes up especially in the issues of judgment, rewards, punishment, and the afterlife. It's not my preferences that matter in such an instance, but God's. If God wanted to require that I constantly wear a red shirt to make it to "heaven," well that would be His prerogative. It would do me no good to protest this, complain about it, or wish it away. Whatever his requirements are is what they are. So, if I were absolutely sure that God required something of me to preserve my existence, I would be a fool not to do it. The question then becomes this: what can I know about God's character, His values, His demands, and His requirements for my appropriate and best response to Him? The issue then focuses on finding out exactly what God wants from me. In other words, what is the truth about God and His desires, and where can I find these answers? They're found in the Bible.

When viewed in this light, it should be evident that not all religions or "religious ideas" are equal. The relative strength or worth of a particular religious idea should be weighed in the context of whether it matters to God, not whether it matters to me. God alone is the objective verifier of ideas about Him and about how we should relate to Him. In the context of our relationship to God, once we presume the existence of God as a personal, sovereign being, it follows logically that the rules of that relationship (every relationship has rules) are made by

Him, not us. Religion is not "all about me" and neither is my relationship to God. It's much closer to "it's all about Him" than anything else.[25] Our goal should be to find out as much as possible about God, His values, and His rules to become adept at compliance, for it would be right and fair in an objective sense.

So, which religious book comes closest to the truth about God? Now, this is a legitimate question. Is it the Bible or some other source? There are good reasons for believing the Bible contains the best, clearest, and most accurate ideas about God, and that is an acceptable topic to debate. But, to sidestep the debate and just lump all religions together as "equally good", you may as well be avoiding the topic altogether. You're giving up on the most important principles ever discovered by man in the misguided attempt to avoid upsetting someone.

But, it's this truth about God which changes the world and its cultures. Because the Bible records the truth about God, the people of the world are constantly adapting their lives to conform to this truth once they discover it. That changes culture, because truth changes the way people live, one person at a time.

The Bible records truth in the form of eyewitness testimony about the works of God. This eyewitness testimony by people who were actually in a position to experience and know the truth of the events they recorded was preserved in the record of Scripture. Many of those giving their testimony were persecuted severely for promoting ideas that were unpopular at the time, yet they clung to their testimony in the face of torture and death. In the following chapter, we'll explore why this was important. The Bible has changed the world by recording and preserving these eyewitness accounts of the works of God.

The earliest writers of the Gospels were eyewitnesses of Jesus' life, His ministry, His miracles, His death, and His resurrection. They saw Him give sight to the blind.[26] They saw Him raise Lazarus from the dead.[27] They saw Him multiply a few small loaves and fishes to feed a multitude of 5,000 people.[28] They saw Him heal people who were crippled.[29] They saw and heard Him teach his wonderful truths

> **The Bible has changed the world by recording and preserving these eyewitness accounts of the works of God.**

from God.[30] They saw Him crucified and sealed in a stone tomb. Most importantly, they saw Him alive after He had been killed.[31] They even touched Him.[32] They ate with Him and spoke to Him for nearly a month after he had been crucified.[33] That is amazing, and that's the eyewitness testimony of many people who were willing to be tortured and killed for saying it. No other world religion can claim this!

There is no reason why anyone would even want to believe these things unless they were true. In the early years of the Church, to be a believer in Jesus Christ came with utterly no material benefit. In fact, the early believers suffered tremendous heartache and pain. Yet, people flocked to the faith from all walks of life for one reason and one reason only: the Bible records the reality about God. It is a truth that—once communicated and grasped—changed the world.

EXHIBIT B

PEOPLE HAVE DIED FOR THIS BOOK BECAUSE IT CONTAINS TRUTH

"I am the resurrection and the life. The one who believes in me will live, even though they die."

The Bible makes some clearly outrageous claims. It makes claims that, if true, are of staggering importance. Nobody would die for such a book unless they were convinced it was true, but people have and will continue to die for the words in this book. The Geneva Bible in the collection of the Historical Bible Society is blood-stained on the New Testament title page. We can only guess what happened. Did someone pay a dear price for possessing that book?

Earlier in this book, it was discussed that the organized Church banned the Bible in the native languages of the lay people. Whether from good or evil motives, this was the sad state of affairs in "Christendom" until the 1500s. This slowly changed after the publication of various Bibles and the result of mass production from the invention of the printing press in 1455. "Forbidden books" were suddenly available in significant numbers. The Bible started to become available to the general public around the middle of the sixteenth century.

DYING FOR "NEW" IDEAS OF TRUTH

For a period of approximately 1000 years, the Bible was not available to the public.[1] This is surprising considering that this occurred during a period in Europe when most people were considered Christian. This was the age of "Christendom" when Christianity was the reigning religion of Medieval Europe and the organized hierarchical Church had pretty much undisputed and absolute power in spiritual (and often worldly) matters.

From approximately 500 A.D. to 1500 A.D. the Bible, if it was available at all, was only available in Latin.[2] Latin was the language of scholars so that, whether a scholar was in England or Italy, by speaking and writing in Latin they could understand one another. Before the printing press, books were so expensive that only the wealthy could afford them, and only the

> **As a result, the Bible was not available for the average person to read.**

wealthiest could afford a Bible. For a priest to buy one, it could cost a year's wages and would take roughly an entire year to produce. This was done very carefully by scribes in monasteries who studied and wrote in Latin. So, when the Bible was copied, it was copied in Latin.

As a result, the Bible was not available for the average person to read. The average person couldn't be expected to read or write his own native language, and even if they were one of the few who could, they certainly couldn't read or understand Latin. As a result, people only knew what was contained in the Bible through stories told by the priest or by the many forms of artwork depicting the various Bible stories. This is why there's so much artwork from the time containing biblical themes. It was a way to communicate at least some biblical truth to the masses, but people only had a general idea what was contained in the Bible because they couldn't read it for themselves.

This all changed with the invention of movable type and the printing press in 1455. Suddenly, it was possible to mass-produce information. It was also not long after this that the people were more inclined to learn to read because of the availability of written material to the public.

Once it was possible to print the Bible in larger quantities, it gradually fell into the hands of the public. However, a question eventually arose. In what language shall we print the Bible? It was forbidden by the organized Church to print the Bible in the common language of the people. Only Latin was authorized for the Bible.

As stated in the previous chapter, this slowly started to change in the early 1500s. The first printings of the Bible in the common languages of the people were illegal and considered "forbidden books." Despite being banned, intellectuals and university students were eager to get their hands on these illegal books because they had never seen the Bible before in their native tongue. They were curious to read Scripture for themselves. Many had these books in their possession at the cost of their very lives.

It was very risky to be in possession of the Bible in any language but Latin because, if you were caught, you were tortured and even burned at the stake.[3] But this didn't stop young intellectuals from reading these books, not by any means. By reading the Bible for themselves, the readers were able to clearly read the teachings of Jesus and the early Apostles in great detail and in their own language. This transformed them.

The early sixteenth century was the time period when students in England were carrying these "forbidden books" around. They would often tear out the title page so they could say that they didn't know what they had. They could pretend ignorance. These students were the radicals of the 1500s and they were "radical" for truth! They wanted to read the Bible for themselves instead of being told what it taught by a priest.

Young people crave truth. When they discover it, it transforms their lives and they live according to it. Those English students of the early sixteenth century were such individuals. They embraced the Bible and they acted upon it. They were tortured and even executed for their testimony and for reading the Bible. Their persecutors were "religious" people, none other than Church leaders themselves, threatened by the Bible being in the hands of the public. Punishing them wasn't something that suddenly sprang up in the sixteenth century. The Apostles themselves were tortured and murdered for their testimony. Even before the ministry of the Apostles, many believers were tortured for their testimony. The Apostles, too, were persecuted and killed by "religious" people.

Eventually, all of society in England and Europe became transformed as the Bible found its way into the hands of the common people. It wasn't just the "radical intellectuals" reading the Bible now. By the eighteenth century, most literate people in Europe and the Americas had read the Bible. This transformed all of society and even nations. In fact, the United States was clearly founded on biblical principles

---

Every trial contains some eyewitness testimony.

---

and Christian values. Though not all of the "Founding Fathers" of the United States were Christian (many were Deists), all of them had a thorough familiarity with the teachings of Jesus and the writings of the Bible. This book will not go into the impact that Scripture has had on the world through the United States of America. Many have undertaken to write on this subject. Suffice it to say, that the world would look very different today without the United States, and the United States would look very different, perhaps not even have existed, were it not for the Bible.

THE IMPORTANCE OF EYEWITNESS TESTIMONY FOR TRUTH

Every trial contains some eyewitness testimony. The importance of eyewitness testimony, the testimony of people who were actually present and experiencing an event as it happened, cannot be overstated. To be present when something is happening is to become part of the event itself. The word apostle means "sent out one." The reason they were "sent out" to speak is because they were witnesses. That is who the apostles were, and their main purpose was to provide eyewitness testimony of Jesus. They were there when Jesus turned water into wine to save embarrassment to a wedding host in Cana.[4] They were present in the boat when Jesus calmed the turbulent sea, saying among themselves, "What manner of man is this that even the wind and the waves should obey him?"[5] They were present when Jesus came walking on the surface of the sea and one of them, Simon Peter, joined him in this physics-defying act at Christ's beckoning.[6] They saw the dead raised (Lazarus) after being buried for four days;[7] they saw His prophecies come to pass;[8] they saw Him heal the deaf, the mute, and the blind. Ultimately, they saw Him crucified and, after initial discouragement and despair, saw Him resurrected from the dead.[9] They were deeply affected by Jesus' life and His words.

If anyone on earth knew the truth about Jesus, it was surely these men and women. They were solemnly charged with the duty and responsibility to "go into all the world and preach the Gospel to all people."[10] This they did, at the ultimate cost of their own lives, as all but two of the original disciples were martyred and suffered greatly for their cause. The exceptions were Judas (who betrayed Jesus) and John the Beloved, who lived in exile (as punishment) to a ripe old age, continuing to minister and spread the "good news" of Jesus' teachings through his writings.

According to scholars, Judas' betrayal of Jesus seems to have been motivated by disillusionment.[11] Like many others, Judas apparently expected Jesus to be a political deliverer who was going to liberate the nation of Israel from its hated Roman oppressors (that was the expectation of the era concerning the Messiah). When Jesus explained that His kingdom was "not of this world"[12] and that His mission was different than the prevailing Jewish expectation, Judas seems to have grown disillusioned with Jesus. It's believed that Judas only expected Jesus to be arrested and imprisoned. When Jesus was put to death, he attempted to return the bribe money, blurting out that he had "betrayed innocent blood."[13] Judas appeared to have felt tremendous remorse because, within days of Jesus' crucifixion, he hanged himself.[14]

No matter how you examine it, all of Jesus' followers reacted strongly to the events He experienced. As a result, they came into conflict with those among the authorities who did not believe—and they suffered greatly.

You might wonder, "Why did God allow his closest friends and his closest beloved followers to be tortured for their testimony and die these horrible deaths?" According to Church tradition, Peter was crucified upside down.[15] We know from the Book of Hebrews that some men of God were sawed in half, some were boiled in oil, and even those who avoided execution were flogged mercilessly.[16] Why did God allow this to happen? Shouldn't He have protected them? Why did God permit this evil?

I think this happened for a very simple reason. If it hadn't, then 2,000 years later any skeptic could say, "They made this all up; they really didn't really see a risen Christ." They could suggest that this was all a big conspiracy, a big lie. These events were so important for the history of the world that there had to be an extreme demonstration of their validity. The story had to be told in a dramatic way or it wouldn't stand the test of time.

In a day when there were no video cameras, the only way the testimony of these eyewitnesses could be transmitted was in writing. The writing would only be believed if the authors paid a large price. They certainly did. It's highly unlikely that anyone would be part of a scam that they knew would result in torture or cost them their lives. As far as we know, only John the Apostle lived to an old age on the Island of Patmos in exile; all of the other Apostles were brutally tortured and executed. That underscores the truthfulness of their witness. They clung to their testimony right up to death.

Now, I'm a lawyer, and I cross-examine people for a living. If you just ask people a few tough questions on the witness stand, they often crumple like a cheap suit. All it takes is just a few pointed questions to expose the truth. Imagine if I had an instrument of torture in my hand and approached a witness. I would easily get the truth out of them! Nobody is going to lie in the face of something like that. But the disciples all went to their deaths and suffered great

> Now, I'm a lawyer, and I cross-examine people for a living. If you just ask people a few tough questions on the witness stand, they often crumple like a cheap suit.

persecution while proclaiming, "We have seen the risen Christ."

"We are not followers of cleverly invented fables,"[17] wrote the Apostle Peter. The Bible tells us he and the Apostles "were eyewitnesses of His majesty."[18] John writes: "That which we have heard, which we have seen with our eyes, which we have looked at and our hands have touched—this we proclaim..."[19] It was the blood of the witnesses that sealed the truthfulness of their testimony. Tertullian, an early Church "father" (and likely a lawyer) wrote, "The blood of the Martyrs is the seed of the Church."[20] He was right.

Even in trial law, in the laws of evidence we have the principle of a "dying declaration." A dying declaration is a particular form of evidentiary testimony that is afforded a high level of veracity if heard by a bystander. Thus, even though it is technically "hearsay" (the dead person cannot appear in court to tell us), it's considered reliable evidence if reported by a third party. A third party can stand up in court and testify, "I heard this. Smith said, while he was dying from the car accident, 'But I had a green light.'" This is allowable evidence and considered reliable in a modern court.

Why? The answer is that when someone is dying or under extreme pressure, it's unlikely they will lie about the last thing they say. That principle validates much of the testimony of the Apostles. What is the point, in the face of death and torture, to give false testimony about Jesus? There is none. Almost all of the early witnesses suffered this fate and not one of them recanted their testimony about Jesus, His life, His miracles, or His resurrection. Doesn't that tell you something?

> **Why? The answer is that when someone is dying or under extreme pressure, it's unlikely they will lie about the last thing they say.**

How exactly was this eyewitness testimony recorded? That's an important question. When was this all written down? Another important question. Let's examine them. The New Testament is so unlike any other religious books which were written hundreds of years after the facts occurred. Let's take the Qur'an, for example. The Qur'an has differing accounts about the way Jesus died.

Muhammad says in the Qur'an that Jesus was never crucified. But later Muslim scholars state that Judas was crucified in place of Jesus and Jesus escaped to Heaven.[21] But, Muhammad wasn't even born when these events happened! Muhammad was 600 years after the death of Jesus. This is undisputed historical fact. He didn't witness any of the events of the Bible. His "testimony" about Jesus would not even be permitted in a court of law. He was never in a position to know the events of Jesus' life.

WERE YOU IN A POSITON TO KNOW THE TRUTH?

Witnesses must be in a position to observe (see and hear) the events to which they testify. That was the test for the apostles. They literally were witnesses to these events. Together, they wrote a good portion of the New Testament and described in detail the life, ministry, death, burial, and resurrection of Jesus.

In spite of this, it's interesting to note that, in the Qur'an, Mohammed writes more about Jesus than he writes about himself. A single individual named Mohammed wrote the Qur'an, though Muslim sources claim that Mohammed was illiterate ("unlettered").[22] We must assume, then, that he authored the Qur'an by dictating it to others. Mohammed was a man who married a wealthy businesswoman and was not particularly fond of Christians and Jews. His book contains "testimony" at odds with the New Testament. Given Mohammad's animosity toward Christians, it's no wonder that he said so much about Jesus that is at odds with the Gospels. The question then becomes, who would you rather believe? Mohammed, writing 600 years after the fact, a single voice who is not a contemporary of Jesus and who had "issues" with Christians and Jews? Or, should we believe and accept the eyewitness accounts of Jesus' friends who were present with Jesus and were willing to be tortured and martyred for their testimony? The question answers itself.

As a trial lawyer, the first question I ask a witness is "Where were you on the night of?" If a witness were to respond by saying, "I wasn't born yet," the judge would tell them to sit down because they can't testify. No judge that I know would permit it. It can't be evidence if it wasn't seen or experienced firsthand. Such is Mohammed's "testimony" about Jesus. He simply wasn't there when these events happened. We could contrast that with John who was present at the crucifixion. We know this because, while hanging on the cross, Jesus said to John, "Son, behold thy mother, mother behold thy son"[23] and John writes, "These things were written that you might believe, and that by believing you might have life in His name."[24] Later on in his work, John speaks of being an actual eyewitness.[25]

The Bible is, therefore, very much an eyewitness account. It does not pretend to have mystical knowledge of the facts. The Bible contains practical, solid, firsthand information. It's a historical record in many places. As we saw, Luke was acting as an investigative reporter and interviewed many eyewitnesses for his book. The early disciples were eyewitnesses of miracles and resurrections.[26] The Book of Acts is presented in the form of an eyewitness account written by Luke. He says things like, "We went here," and "We went there." When Luke is absent from the adventure, he changes his writing style to say, "And then they went there," and "Then we met up with them [at such and such a city]."[27] The text itself reads like an eyewitness account. No other so-called religious "holy book" is in this category.

Facts are important here, because facts (truth) motivate behavior. People will die willingly for important beliefs, but they will only do it if they believe those "beliefs" are true. While many people are willing to die for what they believe in (kamikaze fighters in WWII were willing to die for what they believed in, and we know from recent history, people were willing to fly planes into buildings for what they believed in), they were not in a position to actually know whether what they believed was true. The disciples were not in that situation. The apostles and disciples were there. They watched it happen. They knew the facts. Nobody would willingly die for what they know to be a lie. This is a huge difference.

AN UNBROKEN HISTORY OF COMMEMORATION OF TRUTH

Truth gets transmitted unconsciously by actions at times. Our practices of daily living sometimes testify to ancient truths. For close to 2,000 years the Church has celebrated the resurrection of Jesus as a historical fact. This is not just a myth, nor is this a recent message. This was the declaration of the early Church from "day one." This was the first sermon ever preached within days of the crucifixion, death, and resurrection of Christ. Peter preached as follows: "God raised Jesus from the dead, and we are all witnesses of this. Now he is exalted to the place of highest honor in heaven, at God's right hand." This message resulted in 3,000 people believing in this fact when the Apostle Peter preached his first sermon in Acts. It's recorded that, "[t]hose who believed what Peter said were baptized and added to the church that day—about 3,000 in all."[28] This was no small thing. These were Jewish people greatly moved by the testimony of the Apostles.

Anyone in that crowd could have walked over to the empty tomb and checked it for themselves. If a body was produced, the entire movement known as "Christianity" would have abruptly ended right then and there. They could have asked the witnesses who saw Jesus what they experienced (and they probably did). This was the eyewitness testimony of the Apostles of Christ who saw, touched, ate, and walked with the risen Jesus. These were ordinary people who were just as astonished as you or I would be if we were to see a tortured, murdered person come alive after three days of being buried in a tomb.

These events—the arrest of Jesus in the garden, the kangaroo court trial, the false witnesses, the brutal torture, and His crucifixion and ultimate resurrection—were nothing short of astonishing. They all occurred over the course of a few days and left the disciples reeling with anger, confusion, fear; and finally, astonishment and joy at seeing the risen, victorious Jesus. Make no mistake about it, as soon as Jesus was executed and buried, these people were terrified that they were about to be next. They were surely convinced that the whole thing was over and finished and that it would just be a matter of time before they would all be arrested and suffer the same fate. The first thing they did was to hide. They were certain that, if they were caught, they would have to face crucifixion, too. They were terrified, and many of them did pay the ultimate price for their testimony. This is recorded in the New Testament.

It was in this context that the disciple Thomas, notoriously known throughout the centuries as "doubting Thomas," uttered his famous declaration:

> "Now Thomas (also known as Didymus), one of the Twelve, was not with the disciples when Jesus came. So, the other disciples told him, 'We have seen the Lord!' But he said to them, 'Unless I see the nail marks in his hands and put my finger where the nails were, and put my hand into his side, I will not believe.' A week later his disciples were in the house again, and Thomas was with them. Though the doors were locked, Jesus came and stood among them and said, 'Peace be with you!' Then he said to Thomas, 'Put your finger here; see my hands. Reach out your hand and put it into my side. Stop doubting and believe.'"[29]

Jesus had just been publicly executed! All was lost. Thomas wasn't about to risk any more emotional energy on a lost cause. Haven't we all been there? It's all over and done with and it's time to move on. Thomas really wasn't going to believe any more or invest another thought unless he had proof beyond a reasonable doubt that there was real hope, that there was a legitimate and compelling reason to continue the mission, to continue to believe.

Jesus didn't disappoint him. He appeared to him and not only demonstrated the proof Thomas demanded but somehow knew in advance exactly what Thomas needed to be able to believe. God is like that. He meets us where we are. He answers our objections if we sincerely want those answers. God is not afraid to offer us the necessary evidence to give us faith. He is the "author and finisher of our faith."[30] He gives us what we need to believe.

According to Church tradition, Thomas was martyred in what is now India around 77 A.D.

THE TRUTH IS: MY BROTHER IS CRAZY. OR, IS HE?

In the same way, Jesus made a convincing case of His resurrection to his brother. James, the physical brother of Jesus, became a martyr of the early Church. He was beheaded under the authority of the Roman Emperor Nero who was trying to crush this new Jewish sect of Christianity as detracting from emperor worship (because, after all, the emperors considered themselves to be "gods"). Christians could not in good conscience worship the Emperor Nero as a god when they had knowledge of the real and true God who had demonstrated His power by performing miracles and rising forth from the grave.

Thus, they were tortured and persecuted for this belief and for their testimony about Jesus.

James was no exception. He was probably persecuted as the physical half-brother of Jesus and someone who the Roman authorities wished to make an example of. Yet, this same James believed Jesus was a crazy man only a few short years prior to being martyred for his faith. It says it right in the New Testament book of Mark: "Then Jesus entered a house, and again a crowd gathered, so that he and his disciples were not even able to eat. When his family heard about this, they went to take charge of him, for they said, 'He is out of his mind.'"[31]

James obviously did not believe his brother was God in human form. He thought Jesus was crazy! Who could believe such a preposterous idea? If your brother claimed to be God, you would rightly be skeptical, especially if you were Jewish. "Hear O Israel," the Shema goes, "the Lord your God is one God." Jesus couldn't be God, James believed, and so he ridiculed Jesus as someone who was quite obviously out of his mind. It was very difficult for a religiously observant Jew to believe that God would appear as a man (in human form).

> James obviously did not believe his brother was God in human form. He thought Jesus was crazy! Who could believe such a preposterous idea?

Why does the Bible record such negative information about the Lord of Lords, the King of Glory and about his family and the earliest disciples of Christ? Because the Bible is a true historical document that records these events exactly how they happened and doesn't try to whitewash the truth. "It must be so," James thought, "my brother Jesus has lost his mind!" He told him so. Yet, James ultimately suffered a martyr's death for his belief in Jesus and that Jesus was everything that He claimed to be. What accounts for this change of heart by James, the physical and very skeptical half-brother of Jesus?

The answer can only be that James saw and experienced the resurrected Jesus! He knew his brother had been killed for claiming to be God. That was public knowledge—everyone in Jerusalem knew what happened. He knew the Roman authorities had done a thorough job in the execution of Jesus. They always did. They were experts at torture and execution. He was probably saddened by this fact, but not at all surprised. He may even have thought that Jesus brought it upon Himself for his strange and crazy statements. What better way to get yourself in trouble in ancient Rome than by claiming to be a "god"? Maybe he even thought, "Jesus may be my brother, but he was clearly out of line by making such outrageous claims."

The only explanation for James' 180-degree turnaround was that he experienced the resurrected

Jesus Christ.[32] That would make you a believer! Only that could change your mind. Seeing your brother raised from the dead after being executed would make you a true believer, right? Suddenly, it all fell into place for James. As hard as it was to accept, Jesus was indeed the fulfillment of all the Jewish Scriptures and prophecies. Jesus really was the Messiah, the King of the Jews. Jesus was who He said He was, even though James could not believe it at first. The Bible records all of this.

James eventually goes on to be leader of the early Church in Jerusalem, of all places. This was right where the crucifixion happened! Jerusalem was the center of Judaism, the religion that, for the most part, rejected Jesus' claims. The Jewish leadership had instigated the death of Jesus by turning Him over to the Romans and demanding his execution. James was risking his life by becoming a Christian and a pastor (shepherd of the flock), especially in Jerusalem where sentiments ran so strong. He ultimately paid dearly for it. He was arrested and killed. James was willing to die for his testimony, recorded in the Bible, that Jesus was not a mere man, but the Son of God (and God in human form).

Paul states the importance of the resurrection as foundational for all of Christianity. He doesn't pull any punches, either, when he says that without the resurrection we are the most miserable of all men, believing in vain and having false hope. Here is what Paul writes in 1 Corinthians 15:

> "And if Christ has not been raised, our preaching is useless and so is your faith. More than that, we are then found to be false witnesses about God, for we have testified about God that he raised Christ from the dead...And if Christ has not been raised, your faith is futile; you are still in your sins. Then those also who have fallen asleep in Christ are lost. If only for this life we have hope in Christ, we are of all people most to be pitied. But Christ has indeed been raised from the dead, the first fruits of those who have fallen asleep."

Yes, Christ has indeed been raised from the dead! Otherwise, we have all wasted our time and energy. We celebrate this resurrection 52 times per year, every year, and have done so for almost two thousand years. Every Sunday is "The Lord's Day."

THE SABBATH: WHAT DOES IT TAKE TO CHANGE A HOLY DAY?

The early Christians greatly risked their lives by standing out as a separate group. They were willing to die simply for changing the Sabbath from Saturday to Sunday. While Jews were protected in their religious observances in ancient Rome, Christians were not. They were "fair game" for persecution, torture, and execution. In spite of this, they went out of their way to celebrate Jesus every Sunday as the new Sabbath. This was the equivalent of shining a spotlight on their beliefs. It got them killed. Most Christians, to this day, celebrate the resurrection of Jesus every Sunday. It's the reason why Christians go to church on Sunday instead of any other day. In this way, the resurrection of Jesus Christ is celebrated each and every Sunday in every church throughout the entire world.

The celebration of church on Sunday is actually proof that the resurrection occurred! Here's why. The early Christians were almost entirely Jewish believers who accepted Jesus as the Messiah in fulfillment of all of the prophecies in the Jewish Scriptures (the "Tanakh").

All of the Apostles and early disciples were Jewish. Paul was Jewish. Every writer of the New Testament was Jewish except for Luke (a Greek). The Messiah was a Jewish concept for Jewish people and it all happened in Judea, a Jewish place, and in Jerusalem, the consummately Jewish city. Now, the Jewish people always celebrated the Sabbath (holy day of rest) on the last day of the week (Saturday). This was thoroughly ingrained in Jewish law such that it was even a crime to "break the Sabbath" by doing any work on that holy day of rest. The Sabbath ("Shabbat" in Hebrew) was serious business. "Remember the Sabbath day (Saturday) to keep it holy" was one of the Ten Commandments given by God.[33] It was so important that it made the "top ten" list of what God wanted his people to do. No religious Jew would ever disregard the command to keep the Sabbath. To this day, entire Jewish neighborhoods shut down on Saturday, for Sabbath observance. The Sabbath observance was quite literally "engraved in stone."

The "Sabbath" being Saturday is so ingrained in historical European culture that the Italian word for Saturday is "sabato," which is a clear reference to the word "Sabbath." This is similar to other European languages such as Spanish and Portuguese ("sabado"). Even the etymology of the modern Italian word for "Saturday" shows how closely correlated the Sabbath is to that day of the week. It would take a big historical event to change the meaning of a day so deeply ingrained in culture. Something major must have happened to cause Jewish believers in Jesus to stop worshipping on Saturday and instead substitute Sunday in its place; something so monumental that it would cause a complete change in their Sabbath observance from Saturday (the last day of the week) to Sunday (the first day of the week).

What could have been so dramatic that it caused an entire group of people to change their religious observances of one of the most sacred of all commandments? It could only be changed by an act of God. It had to be the Resurrection of Messiah! The resurrection of Jesus occurred on a Sunday. Sunday came to be known as "the Lord's Day," even by the earliest Jewish believers in Jesus. It was called "the Lord's Day" because it was on that first Easter Sunday that Jesus resurrected bodily from the grave, proving His claims once and for all. Only an event like this could change the Sabbath from a Saturday to a Sunday. By this event, believers knew that God had ordained it. The Sabbath was now Sunday, "The Lord's Day." It has remained so for 2,000 years.

> **The Sabbath was now Sunday, "The Lord's Day." It has remained so for 2,000 years.**

John, a Jewish believer, disciple, and Apostle of Jesus Christ, writes, "I was in the Spirit on the Lord's day..."[34] By this he means, "On Sunday, I was praying..." Note that he calls Sunday "The Lord's day"! This was in the first century AD; and while John, one of the witnesses present at the crucifixion of Jesus and then afterwards, a witness to the resurrected Jesus, was clearly still alive. This was a very early recorded message by a very Jewish man.

Also, in the Book of Acts, even before John's writing, it is recorded that the Church met on the first day of the week: "[o]n the first day of the week, when we met to break bread..."[35] The "bread" reference is to the Lord's Supper (communion), most likely. The Sabbath is changed from Saturday to Sunday! It is now "the Lord's Day." It has been the Lord's Day ever since! Early Christians died so that Sunday would be recognized as "The Lord's Day."

CONFLICT AND OPPOSITION OVER TRUTH

People continue to die for the Bible to this very day. The Bible produces strong reactions in people. It's the only book that has been praised, cursed, restricted, banned, burned, desecrated, and fought over from its beginning right up to the present day. People swear at it and on it. You can't really say that about any other book in the world. Even the fact that Jesus is a "curse" word in some circles is a testimony to the greatness of God. Ironically, that is actually an indirect proclamation of God's deity! The fact that His name is considered blasphemy by some is perversely testifying that He, Jesus, is indeed Lord! Nobody is stubbing their toe and yelling "Buddha," "Vishnu" or "Mohammed!" Even that is telling us something.

The Bible is still banned in some countries today. Possession of a Bible still involves a death sentence in some places. Yet, people are still willing to risk their lives just to have a Bible. For decades in the former Soviet Union, right up to the fall of communism, it was illegal to own a Bible. Today, it is illegal to own a Bible in North Korea, Saudi Arabia, Iran, or Pakistan. The power of the Bible is such that evil, despotic rulers are afraid of its

> **The Bible is still banned in some countries today. Possession of a Bible still involves a death sentence in some places. Yet, people are still willing to risk their lives just to have a Bible.**

message. It elevates people who would otherwise be enslaved. It's a book that is hated and loved simultaneously. It's really not possible to be indifferent toward the Bible. Why? What makes the Bible so powerful is that it makes monumental claims. It claims to be the Word of God over 2,000 times.[36] It says things like, "Thus saith the Lord."[37] That's an outrageous and very strange claim that's either true or false. There is no middle ground here.

Anything that makes those kinds of statements with that regularity has the power to influence the world, and thereby invites a lot of criticism. There's always someone that wants to take a swing at the Bible. There are people who would love to try to undermine that claim. They think,

"If we could just prove the Bible wrong in one respect, then we can discredit the whole thing." "If we succeed," the thinking goes, "it shows that we are smarter than and superior to the Bible!"

To them, I say, "Good luck with that!" People who have challenged the Bible are repeatedly proven to be wrong. Most of the alleged inconsistencies in the Bible are easily explained. The Bible makes monumental claims: people coming back to life from the dead, the promises of eternal salvation for people who believe in Christ's sacrifice on the cross, and other magnificent promises like Heaven, miracles, and healing. There are entire television and radio stations dedicated to the truths of the Bible, not to mention schools, colleges, and universities.

Speaking of which, the first universities were all based on the Bible. Universities, a Christian invention, sought to unite all knowledge under the "universe" of theology, truth about God.[38] Theology was once called "the Queen of Science" for this reason.[39] Every other branch of knowledge, including science, was made possible under the umbrella of the university of God's truth.[40] Modern science has its foundation in biblical truth. It was the concept that God had created an ordered world with natural laws of creation and mathematics that gave a natural basis upon which to seek out and test theories. Much has been written on this and this book will not attempt to deal with that subject. Suffice it to say that almost all of the original scientists were either Christians or Jews. It's not surprising, then, that the vast majority of discoveries, innovations, and inventions to come out of Europe (and the New World) were firmly rooted and grounded in the Bible. How ironic it is now that it's actually a "biblical worldview" that enables science to exist.

Because of the Bible, the standard of living for humans has been raised due to radical discoveries and innovations. Because of the Bible, governments have been toppled, kings have been deposed, and most importantly, lives have been changed. People have given their lives for the Bible, in service of the teachings of the Bible and to the general welfare of the world. The Bible motivates people to some amazing deeds and accomplishments. People are still willing to die for this Book.

REJECTION WITHOUT REASON

Persecution and ridicule continue to this very day because of the Bible. This story is from my personal experience and, while it didn't result in any martyrdom, had this occurred in a different time period it very well may have. The point remains, however, that the Bible provokes intense hostility to this very day.

I was recently present at a brain injury seminar. Brain injuries, especially concussions, are being studied with increasing intensity. These studies are resulting in many new breakthroughs in the understanding of brain injuries and the effects of concussion on the brain. The mechanism and the extent of such injuries are being studied carefully, using technology that was never available before. Injuries that were previously thought to be mild have been found to be anything but, and are affecting people (my clients) in significant ways.

At a conference in New Orleans I attended a particular seminar with several members of my staff and a number of colleagues from across the country that wanted to increase their understanding of how these injuries work on our clients and how they can be proven in a court of law. For a trial lawyer, proving the nature and extent of such injuries using modern technology and diagnostic methods is very important. It was very interesting and highly informative to hear and see a number of qualified and highly-credentialed scientific and medical experts teach authoritatively about their particular niche of study.

During the dinner break after the first evening of the conference, a number of lawyers got together at a local restaurant. There were about twelve of us sitting at this table, enjoying friendly camaraderie and relaxing together after a long day of learning. Someone at the table mentioned that I was interested in the Bible and had spent a good deal of time studying it.

Before I could say anything, the Bible provoked a strong response. Another lawyer sitting next to me, an otherwise intelligent trial lawyer, turned to me and with vehemence said loudly, "The Bible is all a bunch of bull..." Until that moment, we had been politely talking about the seminar. I was stunned at the suddenness and force of her words. Never one to leave a statement like that unchallenged, I politely asked her in everyone's presence why she believed that.

Instead of giving me a clear and reasonable explanation for her beliefs, she proceeded to say over and over again, "The Bible is all a bunch of bull..." I kept pressing her and attempted to engage her in some type of clear debate or discussion, because now the rest of the table was listening. She managed to eke out that "it is all a bunch of fairy tales" and then continued to repeat her phrase of choice. It was rather strange for a trial lawyer, one who specializes in understanding and presenting evidence to prove a point, to base her entire belief system on a premise ("the Bible is a bunch of bull...") without any reasonable basis upon which to hold to that belief.

But here's my point: she could not articulate a single sentence to explain why she felt or believed what she was saying. It was amazing. We were attending an intellectual conference where people came from all over the world to present reasons for why they understood or believed a particular thing. We were all there for that reason, to learn facts and ideas about an important subject that was of professional interest to us; but when it came to the Bible, all that could be said—and said with vehement (but unfounded) conviction—was "The Bible is all a bunch of bull...!" It was ignorance on steroids!

The Bible often provokes reactions like this, even among otherwise intelligent and reasonable people. This woman, an accomplished trial lawyer, had no articulate or reasonable basis for her strong assertion. Her belief is at odds with centuries of human understanding and the vast majority of Western history. She should at least have been able to present some reason why she believes this, but she did not. Her response was purely emotional, guttural, and primal. It was clear that she hated the Bible, but I'm not sure that she even knew why. I don't know her well enough to tell you her personal story, but it was clear that somewhere along the line she had developed a strong dislike—even hatred—for the Bible and people who believe it. She didn't even give me a chance to talk and reason with her.

I think that many people are like that when it comes to the topic of the Bible or religion. They don't give it a fair hearing. They've made up their minds with little or no facts, and they refuse to listen to the evidence. Usually, when someone's lifestyle of choice differs from the Bible, they resort to condemning the Bible rather than examining themselves. Maybe that was the case here. Had this been in a different time period this might have ended badly for me, perhaps with imprisonment or torture.

I think part of the reason for this type of response is a lack of understanding of what Christianity is truly all about. Much of this is the fault of the Church. When I say, "the Church" I am not attacking any particular denomination or organized religion, but what we would call the "Church Universal." The various branches of Christianity are at odds with one another instead of being united. Most of the reason for this disunity is the elevation of differences in the practice of Christianity to the point where it severs fellowship with others who disagree. Styles of worship, theological systems, methods of baptism, the continuation of miracles, supernatural gifts, and other such topics are often the basis for these various differences in denominations. But remarkably, the various branches of Christianity all share most, if not all, of the same basic important beliefs. The core of what we call "the orthodox essentials of the faith" is present in all true Christian denominations.

Many people think of Christianity as just another religion, rather than as the objective truth about God and His plan of redemption for the world. The Church has largely failed in its attempts to communicate what the Bible is truly all about. The Church has allowed the world to define its message rather than being clear about communicating the message of the Bible.

As a result, many people have a stereotypical view of Christianity as medieval Catholicism in which corrupt priests control the people by withholding salvation unless the rules are followed and the organized Church is obeyed. I can understand the frustration with and the rejection of this type of belief system. In a day of extreme personal license and freedom, nobody wants to be told how to live, especially by a bunch of people they perceive as corrupt and who don't even follow their own rules. Protestants are no better. Neither side of the Catholic/Protestant divide has a monopoly on being hypocritical. Christianity is lived one person at a time, not by denominations, and organized religion is often neither "organized" nor "religious."

Things were no different in Jesus' day, by the way. Jesus came largely to rebuke and correct the abuses of religion. For his trouble, He was given a death sentence and crucified by organized religion, working in conjunction with the corrupt Roman local government. Neither the government nor the prevailing religious leaders could tolerate Jesus, who preached the love and acceptance of all people and freedom from the rules of man with spiritual accountability only to God. Jesus told the religious elite that the sinners and prostitutes were entering the Kingdom of Heaven before they were

(Matthew 21:31)! Clearly, Jesus had a "come one and all, just as you are" message. His message was "Come as you are, and I will change you." There's no need to try to fix yourself first. God does it for us.

So, what's the real message of Jesus and the Bible? I can tell you that Christianity is different from every single other religion in the entire world since the invention of this thing called religion. And yes, religion that is not accurate about God is an invention of man. There are many competing inventions about God. Christianity is unique. All religions except Christianity offer a scheme of conduct or practices meant to appease God (or the gods) in an attempt for man to obtain fulfillment, self-actualization, or some type of eternal life. Every single one of these religions is the same in this respect, except Christianity. Every other religion offers a formal code or a practice to ingratiate yourself with the supreme deity to achieve that desired result. They are all exactly the same in this one way. Only Christianity is different.

Christianity is the only religion in which God reaches down to mankind to save us, rather than us trying to save ourselves by performing an act or a service to God in exchange for some benefit. Christianity is the only religion that teaches the grace of God to such an extent that we are saved and redeemed through no effort of our own. It's the only religion that promises the desired result of salvation because of our relationship with God, based purely on an act of God's grace, without any effort or performance on our own part. God rescued us by his own acts and on his own terms.

Although Christianity has rules, salvation is not based on these rules. It's not based on performance. It's not based on works of righteousness, although no one should ever doubt that righteous works are important to do. It's not even based on knowledge, although some knowledge is necessary here because one needs to know about the good news of God's plan to accept it. Christianity, when properly understood, is purely based on God's gift of Himself to mankind without any conditions being met on our part. Christianity is grace, and nothing but pure grace, on the part of the God who loved us so much that He gave Himself up for our salvation. God knew that we could never save ourselves, so He simply went and did it for us. That is the unique aspect of Christianity that separates it from every other religion in the world.

For whatever reason, this message of hope, love, and forgiveness makes people hate you and, at times, want to kill you. In times past, up to and including the present time, people have been willing to die for this message. People have willingly died for the message of truth found in the pages of the Bible.

EXHIBIT C

THE NEW TESTAMENT
IS THE MOST
ACCURATE BOOK
OF ANTIQUITY

"Many have undertaken to draw up an account of the things that have been fulfilled among us, just as they were handed down to us by those who from the first were eyewitnesses and servants of the Word. With this in mind, since I myself have carefully investigated everything from the beginning, I too decided to write an orderly account for you, most excellent Theophilus, so that you may know the certainty of the things you have been taught."

—Luke 1:1–4

The third reason why the Bible is the most important book of all time is that the Bible, especially the New Testament, is the most accurate book of antiquity. That's impressive considering how old it is. Age matters! The New Testament was written in the first century. That's almost 2,000 years ago. When these words were written, people immediately understood them to be important information about God. Did you know that some of the writings of the Bible were considered the actual holy words of God while the writers were still alive?

Other so-called "holy books" were not considered to be Scripture in their religion until after hundreds of years had passed. It took a lot of time for those legends to develop into the status of "holy writ." The Bible is completely different. Peter considered Paul's writing to be "Scripture" while Paul was still alive and the ink was barely dry. You can look at 2 Peter 3:16 for proof.

This is true, even though Peter and Paul were two Apostles that didn't always get along. The New Testament indicates that at various times they were in conflict with one another. Despite their personal squabbles, Peter still held Paul's written words to be Scripture!

The Bible is old. The newest parts of the Bible are 2,000 years old, and many different types of people, not just a single individual, wrote the various books within it. As a result, the Bible has many intellectual viewpoints represented and they all come together in remarkable unity. Together, they present a comprehensive multi-dimensional view of God from various perspectives as, say, multiple witnesses to an event in court might describe the same people or events from different vantage points using their own words.

When the events and testimonies in the Bible are taken together, they form a dynamic whole that provides a living picture of God in action, as we can best understand Him. They do not answer all our questions about God, as God is far too big a subject to ever be completely known or understood. But, they do give us what we need to know about God here and now on Earth. This is called revelation, meaning that God "reveals" as much about Himself as He wants us to know. Taken as a whole, the Bible forms the sum total of God's revelation (revealing) of Himself to mankind.

Much can be expanded and implied from what has already been written in the Bible. We can even draw further conclusions about the nature and character of God based on what is already known. This is what theologians, preachers, ministers, and laypersons do (to the best of their respective abilities). All of this involves some interpretation and, especially, honest sincerity on the part of those who do the interpreting. Theologians call this effort of pulling truth from the Bible "exposition." Theologians must use correct "exegesis." Exegesis is pulling truth out of the text from what is already there rather than reading into the text ("eisegesis") something that is not there.[1] There is so much scholarship on these topics that a consensus has developed as to the meaning of even the most difficult passages of the Bible. As the Bible itself says, "no Scripture is of private interpretation."[2]

CORROBORATION BY OTHER SOURCES

The Bible is accurate when it comes to the people, places, and events it describes. Whenever there is an important archeological discovery, it inevitably confirms the words of the Bible. According to Biblical scholar and professor Dr. Walter C. Kaiser, Jr., "[t]he past century or so has witnessed some of the most remarkable archeological discoveries of the Christian era... archeology has strengthened the case for Biblical reliability."[3] Missing places, people, and events mentioned in the Bible have been corroborated by these archeological discoveries. Some examples of archeological discoveries that have confirmed Biblical narratives are:

1. The discovery of information confirming Sargon, King of Assyria in the 8th century BC (mentioned in Isaiah 20:1), in 1843 by Paul Emile Botta.

2. The confirmation in 1929 of the Bible's assertion that King Belshazzar was the final ruler of Babylon (and not Nabonidus, as scholars had contended).

3. The discovery of the Hittite Empire in 1906 by Hugo Winckler.

4. The discovery of the Horites as a people group (mentioned in Genesis 36:20 and Deuteronomy 2:12, 13) in 1995 by Giorgio Buccellati.

5. The confirmation of the Biblical place of Ophir (from which gold was brought to Solomon), confirmed by an inscription on a piece of pottery found in 1956 referring to "gold of Ophir for Beth-Horon, thirty shekels."

6. An ossuary (bone burial box) discovered in 1990 confirming Caiaphus as a High Priest. He was the one mentioned by the Bible to have presided over the mockery of a trial that was given to Jesus prior to his crucifixion.[4]

The argument traditionally leveled at the Bible is that some of its writings are so old that they cannot possibly be accurate. These discoveries continue to prove that the Bible, despite being ancient, has remarkable accuracy. God has preserved the truth of his Word and we continue to make new discoveries that confirm this. What's even more significant, is that there is not a single discovery that has proven the Bible wrong, despite many centuries of trying.

The Bible can also be verified by external non-religious sources. We have early Roman writings that verify the Bible. Lawyers call that corroboration. I recently acquired the first English translation of Josephus from 1602. This book has in it the testimony called the "Testimonium Flavianum," a testimony written by Josephus in 93 AD about Jesus. It is very close to the events of Christ's life. Here is what it says:

> "Now there was about this time Jesus, a wise man, if it be lawful to call him a man, for he was a doer of wonderful works, a teacher of such men as receive the truth with pleasure. He drew over to him both many of the Jews, and many of the Gentiles. He was the Christ; and when Pilate, at the suggestion of the principal men amongst us, had condemned him to the cross, those that loved him at the first did not forsake him, for he appeared to them alive again the third day, as the divine prophets had foretold these and ten thousand other wonderful things concerning him; and the

tribe of Christians, so named from him, are not extinct to this day." (Antiquities 18.3.3)

As far as we know, Josephus was not a Christian. He was a Jew and a Roman. He is considered a "hostile witness" to Christianity. Sometimes, the best evidence for a fact is given by hostile sources. There is no reason for Josephus, a Jew, to even mention Jesus unless he was extremely important. This is especially true given the tumultuous events that were taking place in the first century for the Jewish people (the slaughter of 1.1 million Jews and the destruction of the Holy Temple).

Scholars will debate whether his writing about Jesus is accurate, and over time some of it may have been tinkered with a bit. For the most part, scholars believe the core of it is accurate and clearly points to Jesus being a great teacher that was alive when the Bible says he was. I bring that up because a lawyer friend of mine was debating me once at a party and said, "I don't believe Jesus even existed." I said, "Really?" He said, "Yeah, there's no evidence outside of the Bible." This is a ridiculous claim.

In a recent article in *Decision Magazine*, Norman Geisler, a noted New Testament scholar, stated this: "Beyond the manuscripts, the people, places and events of the New Testament are attested to by noted ancient historians such as Tacitus, Josephus and Pliny the

Younger."[5] He goes on to say that "Tacitus, considered the greatest historian of his day, wrote in his late first-century *Annals* about the burning of Rome in A.D.64 and the presence of the early Christians in the city. In the same pages, he mentions the crucifixion of Jesus by Pontius Pilate—it is the earliest known non-Christian source that cites Christ's crucifixion."[6]

But first of all, why would you throw out all of the testimony of the Bible as evidence? These authors were physically there. Their testimony is actually the best evidence we have. My attorney friend said, "But these people were all believers, we can't trust them." I said, "Lou, if you'd have seen this stuff, you would've become a believer too." I can't imagine anyone seeing a risen Christ and not becoming a believer. You can't throw out their evidence simply because they were believers in what they saw. Often, in trials, witnesses are so shaken by what they see that they become "believers" in the justice of a case. That is normal and to be expected. I've seen witnesses so upset by accidents that they sided with the injured party. Of course, people believe what they see.

I said, "Lou, you're a divorce lawyer. Who are the two most important witnesses in a divorce case?" I'll tell you the answer, even though it's obvious: the husband and the wife. Are you going to tell me that a judge is going to exclude them from testifying simply because they have an interest in the outcome of the case? No way. Often, that's the only evidence in such cases. We don't exclude witnesses just because they're involved in a case's outcome.

But the basic claim my friend made was wrong, anyway. Beyond the Bible, we have plenty of external sources—Josephus, Pliny, and other ancient Roman writings that verify Bible facts. Archeology, culture, history, and geography also corroborate the Bible.

Try having this conversation with some of your own friends at the next party you go to and I guarantee that you'll find your very own "Lou." The skeptics used to say that there was no evidence of Pontius Pilate existing. To them, that was "proof" that the Bible was inaccurate. But, the absence of proof didn't mean that Pilate didn't exist. It only meant that no proof had yet been found of Pontius Pilate beyond the New Testament documents. That should be obvious to every thinking person. The absence of proof is not proof of absence. Then, in 1960, two Italian archeologists found a plinth (a large ancient stone). It said: "Pontius Pilate: Prefect of Judea."[7] It's hard to get much clearer than that. That argument evaporated overnight.

And how about the Hittites? The Bible talks a lot about the Hittites in the Old Testament, but for a long time we couldn't find a trace of that civilization anywhere. A lot of people refused to believe in the Bible because we couldn't find proof of the Hittites, but guess what happened? In the twentieth century, we found the Hittites. Now, the existence of the Hittites is generally accepted as historical fact.[8]

Every new discovery about the Bible confirms the accuracy of the Bible. Clearly, there are certain things that we'll never be able to prove with complete certainty. The Bible is like an old friend in that, where it can be verified, it's always proven to be true.

LEGALLY-ADMISSABLE EVIDENCE

In legal terms, according to the rules of evidence, the Bible as a document would be considered a "past recollection recorded." Under the Federal Rules of Evidence, a well-known exception to the rule of excluding "hearsay" evidence is codified.[9] This rule is also the rule of evidence in many (if not all) state courts, including New York. It is a rule of evidence which states that a document can be admitted as evidence to prove a fact in court if this document was created at or about the time the events occurred.

The reason? It's considered reliable evidence if a witness made a record, by taking notes or committing something to writing at or near the time the events happened. Thus, if a doctor is treating a patient and is taking a history from the patient and the patient tells the doctor, "I just fell in my bathroom," that statement is admissible in court even if the person who made the statement (in this case the patient) is not in court to testify to it and even if the patient denies saying it in the first place. This is called a "recorded recollection" or a "past recollection recorded."

The Bible is, in many ways, exactly such a document. It contains the recorded recollections of various witnesses at or about the time the events occurred. The Bible also functions like a transcript of a trial in that it records the events being discussed "live and in person" exactly as they were debated by the parties. So, when the Bible writes that the Jewish religious leaders told Jesus he was "demon-possessed" (John 8:48), we see this

> The Bible also functions like a transcript of a trial in that it records the events being discussed "live and in person" exactly as they were debated by the parties.

occurring in real time, in the heat of the battle of Jesus' fiery debate with His accusers. We see (and we feel) the passion of the moment, and we also see Jesus' response to that charge. It's all recorded by eyewitnesses (in this case, John the Apostle).

Not only are "past recollections" admitted into evidence in court as exceptions to the hearsay rule, but other documents containing hearsay are also admitted because they are considered utterly reliable. Documents such as transcripts, public records, records of regularly-conducted activities (repair and maintenance logs), medical records, and many other types of business records are admissible in court even if the person who made the statements in those records is not alive or otherwise present to go to court. We do not need live testimony in court today from the Apostles (they are dead, in any event) because we have reliable written records of their experiences with Jesus.

I have another friend who says that the witnesses to the resurrection of Jesus should have been subjected to cross-examination, as in a court of law. As a lawyer, he believes in the right to confront witnesses and to have them vigorously questioned to make sure that what they said is reliable and not the product of fantasy or ulterior motives. I understand that. As a lawyer, myself, I understand that the right to cross-examine witnesses to expose flaws or weaknesses in their testimony is a great tool and a right of all who are accused. Cross-examination is an indicator of reliability. A challenged witness becomes either more or less reliable when questioned by a hostile source. I have watched untruthful witnesses get so dismantled on the witness stand that, after a vigorous and thorough cross-examination, nothing of what they originally testified about remained valid. Nobody in the courtroom would believe another word they said.

But, I've also seen the opposite from a truthful witness. I've seen witnesses cross-examined for lengthy periods of time and their testimony only got better and stronger the more they were challenged. That's a solid and credible witness. That's the sign of a truthful witness. So, yes, I believe in cross-examination. That's what exposes the truth in testimony.

A skillful, forceful cross-examination will expose any and all weaknesses in a story. We use it all the time. By the way, the first ever recorded use of cross-examination is actually in the Bible. It's in the apocryphal Book of Susannah and the Elders. In that case, two religious leaders (elders) were lying, claiming that a beautiful married woman was eager and willing to have sexual relations with them (when in reality they had raped her). The Prophet Daniel was one of the judges in her trial (she was accused of adultery!), and when he separated the witnesses and cross-examined them with questions, their stories quickly unraveled. The result was that the woman was vindicated and the Elders were found guilty instead. Yes, cross-examination works.

The Apostles were eyewitnesses to the life, the ministry, the miracles, the trial, the death, and the resurrection of Jesus. They testified to this with great boldness in a hostile environment. And they were indeed cross-examined! They were brutally questioned under penalty of death. In Acts 5:29, when they were confronted by hostile authorities and questioned, they said, "We must obey God rather than men." They realized that it was better for them to please God than to please their inquisitors. So, they literally died getting that truth out there for all to hear, for posterity and for us. If that's not cross-examination, then I don't know what is. This brutal cross-examination only solidified their testimony.

TEXTUAL ACCURACY

As far as the accuracy of the biblical text reflecting what the authors actually wrote, there's such an abundance of biblical manuscripts that it's very easy to reconstruct the original text of the Bible. If anything, we have a little bit extra that we're not sure whether it should be included. There are about 40 lines of the Bible that are in dispute, but none of them affect a revelation of God or an important doctrine of the Church in the slightest. Every teaching and principle that is truly important has been stated over and over in so many different ways that it's hard to miss.

There's a professor in North Carolina named Dr. Bart Ehrman. In 2005, he wrote a book called *Misquoting Jesus*. It caused quite a stir. He took what scholars have known for many centuries, which is that there are indeed some copyist errors in the biblical text, and sensationalized that fact. He sold a lot of books this way and made a name for himself.

What Dr. Ehrman suggests in his book is that it's possible that the written Scriptures have been so corrupted by repeated copying and scribal errors, deletions, and additions that we can't possibly be sure we have the accurate transmitted words of the original authors. Thus, his argument goes, since we don't have the original words of the authors (commonly referred to as the "autographa"), it's hopeless to try to rely on the Scriptures in the form we now have in front of us when we open the Bible. He claims that the Bible text has become thoroughly corrupted. This is actually silly.

There is such an abundance of ancient Biblical manuscript evidence that people should be embarrassed to make arguments like this. There's no doubt about what message is being communicated through the Bible. As said earlier, there are approximately 40 lines of text of the New Testament that are in question. Even if you discard those 40 lines, it doesn't change anything that the Bible conveys.

As an example of a disputed text, consider the Gospel of John, Chapter 8. That section of the Bible (we call it a pericope) with the woman caught in adultery is indeed questionable. The earliest and best quality manuscripts don't have that little story. And if you read your Gospel of John and you come to that part in the Scripture where

Jesus confronts the woman's accusers and writes in the dirt, "Let he who is without sin cast the first stone," you should be made aware that the earliest and best-quality manuscripts simply don't have that passage. You can actually see from reading it that it looks like somebody inserted it in that place. The story doesn't follow the general reading or written style of John.

My answer is, "So, what?" That doesn't mean the story isn't true. It just means that the story isn't in the earliest and best manuscripts. If you read the New International Version (NIV) like I sometimes do, you'll see something in the footnotes like "the earliest and best manuscripts do not contain these verses." That's honest, and it's good information, but it really doesn't change a single thing.

To reiterate, this doesn't mean that the passage shouldn't be in the Bible, it just means that this is the truth of what we know about the early documents. We don't need that story, by the way, to know that Jesus is merciful and forgiving. We have evidence of that in many other places. The Bible is purposefully redundant on the important points and Jesus, likewise, always used repetition when He taught. To argue that the entire Bible is corrupted because a few lines are disputed is like saying you can't see the picture of a jigsaw puzzle because one of the pieces is missing.

So, what happened with this story? Most scholars believe that it's a true story, transmitted by oral tradition, and one early scribe who was making a copy of the Book of John said to himself, "Wait a minute! I can't find that story anywhere. I think I'll add it here." We have no way to know for sure. We do know that you don't really need that story to get the message of the Bible, you don't need it to learn about God, and you don't need it to become a redeemed child of God. There's plenty of material in the Bible that is undisputed. In fact, you only need one verse, John 3:16—"For God so loved the world, that He gave his only begotten Son, that whoever believes in him should not perish but have eternal life. For God did not send his Son into the world to condemn the world, but in order that the world might be saved through him." This verse is not in dispute by scholars. This verse is enough for the salvation of your soul. Believe that! Trust that verse and you have enough to meet God someday without fear. There is so much more in the Bible that is undisputed and without a hint of copyist error.

PRESERVATION OF THE TEXT

What about the ancient manuscript evidence for the text of the New Testament? Is there enough proof to show that the text was correctly preserved? Or was the text corrupted?

When it comes to the Bible, we have over 25,000 ancient manuscripts in a significant number of ancient languages. Erasmus translated the Greek New Testament in 1516 with only seven or eight Greek New Testament ancient manuscripts.[10] People criticized this text. They said, "Well, there are some inaccuracies there." There were many more manuscripts in existence, even in Erasmus' day, but he only had access to those few. Since Erasmus produced that volume in 1516, there have been more discoveries of biblical manuscripts—hundreds more— with some dating prior to the 3rd Century.[11] Some even date to the 1st Century, itself.

We have complete New Testament manuscripts from as early as the 4th Century.[12] That is very early in terms of the events recorded. We have fragments going back much, much earlier; some even to the Apostle Matthew's lifetime. That interval, between the events and the earliest fragments, is relatively tiny. The earliest fragment that we have is called "P52" (not an airplane, it identifies the fragment number -"papyrus 52"), a selection from the Gospel of John that was written within years of when Jesus was crucified, buried, and resurrected. It's now believed that in Magdalene College, in Cambridge, England, they may have uncovered an original (autographa!) of the Gospel of Matthew.[13]

In terms of manuscript evidence, the second best-documented ancient work is Homer's *Iliad*. Scholars generally believe that we have an accurate copy of it. Scholars accept this, even though the complete copy that we have is dated to 2,500 years after Homer wrote it, and there are only approximately 1,000 manuscripts.[14] That's actually an abundance of manuscripts for an ancient book. Everyone, including scholars, accepts Homer's *Iliad* to be accurate. So, why is a higher standard being required for The Bible? It makes no difference, though. The Bible exceeds this higher standard, too.

We also have more modern and accurate dating techniques available to us today. The remarkable thing is that every time we find more manuscripts or develop better dating methods, they always end up supporting the texts and making them more accurate. This is why I love the New International Version (NIV) Bible, because it's based on a superabundance of early manuscripts. We call that the "critical text" versus what's called the "majority text."[15]

These are essentially two variants of Greek texts making up the New Testament, and they differ slightly. One called the "critical text" and the other called the "majority text." By way of gross simplification, the "majority text" is the line of New Testament manuscript copies that are related to one another where the vast majority of manuscripts are of the same family "tree." The "critical text" is that line of related manuscripts that dates back to the earliest times of the writings. The "critical text" documents are generally older and more reliable, but don't appear in as many copies as the "majority text." Ultimately, this is just two different ways of grouping the ancient documents. One is by number of documents (majority text), the other is by age (critical text).

It needs to be noted that the average person wouldn't notice much of a difference between any of these manuscripts, regardless of which group they were classified in. It's often just spelling, punctuation, and small differences in writing styles. Since the manuscripts have been discovered, we've been able to cross-match and cross-reference everything and find out exactly where a scribe fell asleep, skipped a line, jumped a word, wrote a word twice, or was simply sloppy. These are the types of errors we're talking about when we say "copyist errors." Many errors are obvious and mean nothing. Only a few really matter and none make any real difference.

One is by number of documents (majority text), the other is by age (critical text).

I tell young people that when you're full of fire and serving God and you get to college, a professor like Dr. Ehrman might point out to you that there are some errors in the Bible. Be ready for that. These God-fearing, Bible-reading young people tell me, "Oh, I thought the Bible was perfect!" Yes, the Bible is indeed perfect as originally written, but there are copyist errors in the later manuscripts. This is an easy challenge for believers to refute. Why? Because it's a deceptive issue and doesn't change anything. The most accurate response is, "So what? We can easily reclaim the original text." It's like your loved one saying to you: "I love you more than anything," rather than saying, "I love you more than any other person." You know what they mean.

For a biblical comparison, we can take a look at all the different translations of John 3:16. You can see for yourself that every variation of the text leads to the exact same message:

New International Version: "For God so loved the world that he gave his one and only Son, that whoever believes in him shall not perish but have eternal life."

Douay-Rheims Bible:
(English College at Rheims and Douay—1609)

> "For God so loved the world, as to give his only begotten Son; that whosoever belie-veth in him, may not perish, but may have life everlasting."

King James Bible (KJV):
(Public Domain/Cambridge University Press—1611)

"For God so loved the world, that he gave his only begotten Son, that whosoever believeth in him should not perish, but have everlasting life."

Webster's Bible Translation:
(Durrie & Peck—1833)

"For God so loved the world, that he gave his only-begotten Son, that whoever believeth in him, should not perish, but have everlasting life."

Young's Literal Translation:
(Robert Young—1862)

"For God did so love the world, that His Son—the only begotten—He gave, that everyone who is believing in him may not perish, but may have life age-during."

English Revised Version (ERV):
(Oxford—1885)

"For God so loved the world, that he gave his only begotten Son, that whosoever believeth on him should not perish, but have eternal life."

Darby Bible Translation:
(J. N. Darby—1890)

> "For God so loved the world, that he gave his only-begotten Son, that whosoever believes on him may not perish, but have life eternal."

American Standard Version (ASV):
(Thomas Nelson & Sons—1900)

> "For God so loved the world, that he gave his only begotten Son, that whosoever believeth on him should not perish, but have eternal life."

Weymouth New Testament:
(The Baker and Taylor Co.—1902)

> "For so greatly did God love the world that He gave His only Son, that everyone who trusts in Him may not perish but may have the Life of Ages."

New American Standard Bible (NASB):

(The Lockman Foundation—1963)

> "For God so loved the world, that He gave His only begotten Son, that whoever believes in Him shall not perish, but have eternal life."

New American Standard Bible (NASB):

(The Lockman Foundation—1977)

> "For God so loved the world, that He gave His only begotten Son, that whoever believes in Him should not perish, but have eternal life."

Aramaic Bible in Plain English:

(Harper & Row—1985)

> "For God loved the world in this way: so much that he would give up his Son, The Only One, so that everyone who trusts in him shall not be lost, but he shall have eternal life."

GOD'S WORD Translation (WORD):
(Baker Publishing Group—1995)

> "God loved the world this way: He gave his only Son so that everyone who believes in him will not die but will have eternal life."

New Living Translation (NLT):
(Tyndale House Foundation—1996)

> "For God loved the world so much that he gave his one and only Son, so that everyone who believes in him will not perish but have eternal life."

American King James Version (AKJV):
(Public Domain—1999)

> "For God so loved the world, that he gave his only begotten Son, that whoever believes in him should not perish, but have everlasting life."

Jubilee Bible (JUB):

(Ankeo Press—2000)

> "For God so loved the world that he gave his only begotten Son, that whosoever believes in him should not perish but have eternal life."

King James 2000 Bible (KJ2000):

(Dr. Robert A. Couric)

> For God so loved the world, that he gave his only begotten Son, that whosoever believes in him should not perish, but have everlasting life."

World English Bible (WEB):

(Rainbow Missions—2000)

> "For God so loved the world, that he gave his one and only Son, that whoever believes in him should not perish, but have eternal life."

English Standard Version (ESV):
(Crossway Bibles—2001)

> "For God so loved the world, that he gave his only Son, that whoever believes in him should not perish but have eternal life."

Holman Christian Standard Bible (HCSB):
(Holman Bible Publishers—2003)

> "For God loved the world in this way: He gave His One and Only Son, so that everyone who believes in Him will not perish but have eternal life."

New English Translation Bible (NET):
(Biblical Studies Press—2005)

> "For this is the way God loved the world: He gave his one and only Son, so that everyone who believes in him will not perish but have eternal life."

New Heart English Bible (NHEB):

(AuthorHouse—2008)

> "For God so loved the world that he gave his only Son, so that whoever believes in him will not perish, but have eternal life."

International Standard Version (ISV):

(The ISV Foundation—2011)

> "For this is how God loved the world: He gave his unique Son so that everyone who believes in him might not be lost but have eternal life."

Berean Literal Bible (BLB):

(Bible Hub—2016)

> "For God so loved the world that He gave the only begotten Son, so that everyone believing in Him should not perish, but should have eternal life."

Berean Study Bible (BSB):
(Bible Hub—2018)

> "For God so loved the world that He gave His one and only Son, that everyone who believes in Him shall not perish but have eternal life."[16]

After reading all these versions, which rely on all the different manuscripts, are you thinking, "I have no idea what's being said"? Of course, you're not. It's deceptive and misleading to claim that the text of the Bible has been corrupted.

In Dr. Ehrman's book, he raises these questions: "Why did God not save for us the autographa? Why do not we have them somewhere?" He would like to have them, and I would, too. But, I suspect that if some person or group of people had these original texts, they would have made an idol out of the texts themselves. They would be charging people to line up just to look at them. To do this would be an abomination. It would also allow one group or person to "own" these special, unique texts. I can't imagine that God would ever sanction that. It's not the original documents that count; it's the message that matters, and the message belongs to everyone.

The Second Book of Kings, Chapter 18, tells the story of the Nehushtan, a bronze serpent on a pole erected by

Moses at God's direction to protect the Israelites when they were in the wilderness. God instructed Moses that the pole would protect the Israelites who saw it from dying by the bites of "fiery serpents" that had been sent by God as punishment. The story itself was prophetic—a savior, a Messiah (meaning, "God Saves"), being "lifted up" on a pole.[17] The pole itself was just a piece of bronze, but over time it eventually became an important artifact, and King Hezekiah decreed that it should be kept in storage. It was an important antique relic. But people went crazy over it! King Hezekiah eventually had to destroy it because people began worshipping it. That's pretty telling about human nature. So, it's probably a good thing, then, that the original texts haven't been located.

The Bible is so accurate that if every single Bible on the planet was destroyed, the Scriptures could be reconstructed from third-party sources alone. In fact, Sir David Dalrymple, a Scottish scholar and judge, did just that for the New Testament in the mid-18th century. From his own library, he was able to reconstruct all of the Scriptures, with the exception of only 11 verses.[18] And clearly, he didn't have every book ever written, and we pretty much do.

As stated earlier, the King James version of the Bible was based on the translations of a mere handful of manuscripts put together by Erasmus in 1516. The King James Bible was printed in 1611. Since that time, there have been numerous large manuscript discoveries that are now available to us for study and translation. Discoveries such as Codex Sinaiticus, Bodmer Papyri, Chester Beatty papyri, and the availability of Codex Vaticanus (in the Vatican Library since 1492, but not available to Erasmus),[19] among other finds, have resulted in such an abundance of manuscript evidence that it is now relatively easy to reconstruct the vast majority of disputed passages. In any event, no disputed passages have ever affected any major thought, practice, or doctrine of Christianity.

But the "accuracy of the text" argument was put ultimately to rest once and for all in 1948 with the discovery of the Dead Sea Scrolls. That is the "smoking gun" evidence that should completely dismantle all arguments made by anyone claiming that the Bible is invalidated by textual error.

You may have heard the story of the shepherd boy in Qumran. He was bored while watching his herd of sheep in the desert. He threw a rock carelessly into a cave and it made an odd sound, like something breaking. He went inside to check it out and he found pottery; and in the pottery, he found ancient manuscripts. Immediately, the Israeli government started looking at other caves, which led them to find other jars, and in total, many hundreds of ancient manuscripts. These are known as the Dead Sea Scrolls and are dated to before the time of Christ. These scrolls were remarkably preserved because of the arid desert climate. I would bet that this is no coincidence.

One of the many works they found is called the Great Isaiah Scroll. The Great Isaiah Scroll is important because it's a complete copy of the Book of Isaiah. When they unrolled it, they were very eager to compare it to our current Book of Isaiah to see if it had changed. The world waited in suspense.

Isaiah probably wrote his book around 700 BC. Before the discovery of the Dead Sea scrolls, the earliest complete copy anyone had of the Book of Isaiah was from 900 AD. That's right around the start of the Middle Ages, long after the time it was written, an interval of 1,600 years!

> **To me, that's the most convincing argument from an evidence point of view that nothing has changed in the documents.**

But now we had new evidence in the Dead Sea Scroll discoveries. The Isaiah Scroll that they found in Qumran was from 100 BC, 1,000 years earlier than our earliest scroll (900 AD). They opened it, unwrapped it, and found that it was nearly word-for-word identical.

To me, that's the most convincing argument from an evidence point of view that nothing has changed in the documents. There were some minor variations of spelling and stylistic differences, but nothing of any real substance. We now know how accurately these documents were preserved. I think that should put to death the copying arguments once and for all. Yes, there were some scribes who were amateurs, but there were also some very professional scribes. We can cross-reference all of this (it was done even before computers) and we know exactly where someone had a slip of a pen or skipped a line. With computers, it's even easier to do now.

To really demonstrate how little these alleged textual changes have corrupted the Biblical text, it would be great if we had a large portion of identical scripture that appears in two totally different books of the Bible. This would mean that every copyist would have copied them at separate times over the years. We could then compare these two identical portions and see how different they are from each other in the final rendering. One would presume that these two (hypothetical) passages of Scripture would be so different from each other that there would be vast differences between them due to copying errors, changes, additions, and/or deletions because each passage would have different mistakes when recopied over the centuries. Imagine if we only had such passages to examine and compare!

It just so happens that there do exist two such identical passages in the Old Testament! They are found in 2 Samuel 22:2-51 (the entire chapter except the first verse) and Psalm 18. Entitled David's "Song of Praise" in the NIV translation of 2 Samuel, this lengthy passage is simply another psalm in the Book of Psalms. In 2 Samuel, this portion of Scripture consists of 166 lines of prose, while in Psalm 18 it is 170. They are not exactly alike, as this reflects changes in the text over the centuries (so-called "copyist errors"). The variations in the passages are likely due to sloppy copying. When comparing one section line-by-line with the other, it is easy to see where a line has been added or deleted and there are slight changes in the meaning.

But here's the point. No intelligent person reading these two separate lengthy passages of Scripture would derive a different meaning or theology from reading one or the other. They undoubtedly started out as identical. Any change in the text is completely inconsequential. These passages are not only in separate books, but also in separate sections of the Hebrew Bible (Samuel would be in the section entitled "Prophets" while Psalms would have been in the section entitled "The Writings").

It is likely that different scribes (copyists) would have copied these passages separately from one another in the same era. This would account for the differences. This would be similar to copyists copying the same passage of the Bible in different eras, except that in this example we might have different copyists copying the same text in different passages of the Old Testament in the same era. The end result is most probably very similar and gives us a great example of how the text was preserved even with different hands over the centuries, because this process would have been repeated each time these passages were copied.

The differences in text are as follows:

First, read 2 Samuel 22: 5–7:
"The waves of death swirled about me;
the torrents of destruction overwhelmed me.
The cords of the grave coiled around me;
The snares of death confronted me.
In my distress I called to the LORD;
I called out to my God,
From his temple he heard my voice;
My cry came to his ears."

Compare the above text with Psalm 18:4–6:
"The cords of death entangled me;
the torrents of destruction overwhelmed me.
The cords of the grave coiled around me;
The snares of death confronted me.
In my distress I called to the LORD;
I cried to my God for help.
From his temple he heard my voice;
my cry came before him, into his ears."

No doubt the copyist's eye must have picked up the wrong line when the word "cords" is used in both the first and second sentence in the latter passage while used only in the second sentence in 2 Samuel. The result is that we have "cords of death entangled me" instead of "waves of death swirled about me." Also, it looks like a line was either skipped in one passage or repeated twice in the second passage. Yet both renderings make the same point, do they not? These are the types of alleged "corruptions" that occur with some small frequency in the Bible.

Some things are not verifiable enough for people to believe the Bible. Clearly, we do not have a video of Christ or the Apostles walking around healing people. Even if we did have such a video of Jesus performing miracles, people would still not necessarily believe it. You can always find a reason not to believe. Many people place unrealistic demands on the Bible simply because they do not want to believe what it says. If they believe it, then they'd have to alter their lifestyle choices. They would have to submit to God and not be their own lord and master. This is a matter of the heart, not of proof. Just as a mother could never sit on a jury and convict one of her children, some people are so biased against the idea of God that no amount of proof will ever convince them.

This, plus slips of the pen, stylistic changes in each era, and spelling errors, make up the bulk of such "corruptions" in the Bible. According to Dr. Philip Comfort, there are really only approximately fifty verses in the entire New Testament where the text is disputed as to whether they were in the original manuscripts.[20] And, as said earlier, none of these variables would affect the theology and practice of God's people. Should we ignore the indisputable text of these remarkable Scriptures because a relatively few passages have copyist errors? I do not think so. You be the judge.

THE LOSERS WRITE HISTORY?

Another reason we know the Bible is accurate is that it recorded negative information about powerful and important people. If you're King David, you're not only a "man after God's own heart;"[21] you're the king! You are the absolute ruler of Israel. You can pretty much do anything.

In fact, King David was so lacking in boundaries that he decided he wanted one particular woman to be his wife even though she was married to another man, a loyal servant of King David. So, he brought Bathsheba, Uriah's wife, to his palace for an evening of illicit sex. It's a famous and well-known story.[22] David got Bathsheba pregnant. Her husband was one of King David's loyal generals and also his neighbor.

> So, you've got everything here—murder, lust, adultery, and cover up. How did this make it into the Bible?

This was a horrible act of betrayal, an act of disloyalty, lust, and adultery. And to make it worse, David lied about it. Then, when he couldn't hide the lie anymore, he had Uriah killed. After all, he was the king. He had Uriah murdered to cover his sin.

So, you've got everything here—murder, lust, adultery, and cover up. How did this make it into the Bible? David could have demanded that all records of this be scrubbed—he was the king! He had absolute power. Why is it in there? Because that's what happened. It's the truth, and God wanted us to know. The Bible tells it the way it is. This horrible story wasn't "sanitized" for David's protection. All the sordid details are there.

How about Peter denying Jesus Christ after making a big boast, saying, "Everyone will deny you, but I'll never deny you"?[23] Peter went on to be the Great Apostle, a powerful leader of the early Church. Some claim he was the first Pope. He really put himself out there with that statement, bragging about his faith and courage!

Jesus said "No, Peter. Before the rooster crows, you're going to deny me three times."[24] Sure enough, before the cockerel could warm up his vocal chords, there was Peter, protesting and denying he ever knew Christ, just as Jesus said he would. The last time he denied it to a little servant girl! A servant girl! He was a real coward in that moment. That also makes it into the Bible. Why? Because that's what happened. It's an accurate description of real events. The Bible tells the truth, even when it's not pretty and even when it concerns the powerful.

Now, Peter certainly was in a position to say "Hey guys, can we leave that part out? It's not all that flattering." And while some may argue that "the winners write history," it doesn't happen in the case of the Bible. It is all in here: the good, the bad, and the ugly. And some of it is really ugly.

How about that part where the Apostle Paul and the Apostle Peter have a nasty argument? Paul stood up to Peter's face, publicly calling him a "hypocrite" because he wouldn't eat with the Gentiles.[25] It's in the Bible. Two Apostles arguing with each other makes it into the text. The truth is recorded.

Here's my favorite: the first witnesses to the Resurrection were women.[26] Did you know that in the 1st Century it was illegal for a woman to be considered a valid witness? A woman's testimony did not count in court. If you were in the first century putting together a list of witnesses for a case, you'd want every important, high-ranking man you could think of. And, if you were making it up, that's who you would claim were witnesses to the event. But, who are the first recorded witnesses to the resurrection in the Bible? Two women, because that's the way it happened.[27]

I'll tell you a little trial lawyer secret. Women actually make the best trial witnesses. They remember everything.

Women know all the details, the colors, and the faces. God, in His wisdom, knew that too, even though it took our society 2,000 more years to figure it out. Of course, there were many other witnesses to the Resurrection, but I find it fascinating that God picked women to be the very first important biblical witnesses for this truth. They may have been illegal witnesses, but they were very good ones!

PROPHETIC PREDICTIONS ACCURATELY FULFILLED

The Bible is considered accurate for many reasons, including prophecies predicted thousands of years in advance of their completion and fulfilled even to the smallest degree. Some people get excited about the prophesies of Nostradamus, a sixteenth century mystic who composed many obscure writings that people have tried to interpret over the years. The problem with the "prophecies" of Nostradamus is that nobody agrees what his words even mean. Different people reading the exact same passage of his works come up with entirely different meanings. Recently, a TV show aired indicating his writings predicted that Hillary Clinton would win the 2016 Presidential Election.[28] I guess Nostradamus blew that one.

The prophecies of the Bible are nothing like that. They are often quite specific. One of my favorite little tricks is to take Isaiah 53 and let somebody read it, usually a secular Jewish person. I'll say, "Read this, and tell me who it's about." They'll read it and say, "Clearly that is talking about Jesus; what's your point? I'm Jewish." I'll say, "The passage is in the Tanakh (the Old Testament). This is your prophet Isaiah! He was describing your Messiah, writing 600 years before Jesus was born. Can you explain that?" Then they either want to hear about Jesus or they want to talk about golf. The prophecies in the passage are truly that accurate.

The fact that everybody reading Isaiah comes to that same conclusion just shows the accuracy of these prophecies. The Book of Daniel is another book of the Bible that is so accurate in predicting the succession of world empires that critics have tried to say that it must have been written after it all happened. Yet, we know that it was copied by the Jewish Greek translators in the Septuagint in approximately 275 BC, clearly before some of the events it predicts.[29]

Another example is found when Jesus was walking with His disciples and pointed to the Temple in Jerusalem and said, "Within a generation, not one of these stones is going to stand upon another."[30] The people who heard this were astonished. His own disciples were astonished. I'm not sure if they really believed Him. Someone said to

Him, "It took 46 years to build this Temple. You're telling us that within a generation it'll be gone?"

That's exactly what He said. And I doubt they really comprehended the importance of that prophecy. But sure enough, in 70 AD, the legions of Titus Vespasian came in, leveled Jerusalem, and set fire to the Temple. The gold in the Temple melted and ran into the cracks between the stones. The Roman legions literally pried every stone apart to get to the gold.[31] That is an amazing fulfillment of prophecy. The destruction of the Temple is a documented historical fact recorded by the Roman (and Jewish) historian Josephus who describes these events, including the Siege of Jerusalem, in great detail.[32]

This prophecy is important for spiritual as well as historical reasons. Why? Because at that point in history, it was clear to those who followed Jesus that the children of God no longer needed a Temple or an altar. They didn't need any further sin sacrifices. The sin sacrifice was made once and for all on the cross by Jesus, Himself. It all fits so nicely into what happened in biblical history. That is why Jesus made a point of predicting it. A Temple is superfluous at this point and has been ever since Jesus died and was resurrected. You don't need a Temple if you don't need any more sacrifices.

The Book of Hebrews says, "The blood of bulls and goats was never going to be able to take away sin."[33] So, we had the once and for all sacrifice who came into the world and died on the cross in approximately 33 AD. In 70 AD, the Temple was demolished by the Romans. God stayed true to his word. It makes perfect sense to me that you don't need a Temple or an altar for sacrifices, and you clearly don't need animal sacrifices anymore. Sacrifices are over, as of 70 AD. No Temple is needed. God's timing is perfect. The prophecy was fulfilled completely.

There are at least 300 separate prophecies dealing with the Messiah that were accurately fulfilled by Jesus of Nazareth.[34] These prophecies include His place of birth being Bethlehem.[35] They include Him coming from the town of Nazareth.[36] They detail His lineage and genealogy and other highly-specific information. There have been books written about the many prophecies concerning Jesus that have been fulfilled. Nobody ever came close to fulfilling these prophecies besides Jesus.

Several years ago, a book was written called *The Passover Plot.*[37] The premise of that weird book was that Jesus purposely attempted to try to fulfill those prophecies to fit the bill and to "be someone." This is a preposterous notion. It was a desperate attempt to explain away how accurately Jesus "fit the bill." Most of those prophecies were beyond anyone's natural ability to fulfill, including the identity of Jesus' mother and historical events that happened during his childhood. You simply can't fake that.

The lineage of Jesus is recorded in Matthew and Luke.[38] Even the tediously-recalled lineage of His ancestors is there for a reason. It is positive proof of the pedigree of Jesus being the Messiah as predicted in advance by the Jewish prophets. If a person arrived on the scene today and claimed to be the Messiah, his claim would have to be bogus. All the records of genealogy were destroyed when the Jewish Temple was destroyed, so there's no way a modern Jewish man could possibly prove descent from the tribe of Judah, or from the line of David, as is the requirement for the Messiah.

THE CREDIBLE WITNESS DOESN'T LIE

The Bible has the "ring" of truth to it. I like to use the example of a friend that, over time, tells you a thousand different things. If you're a skeptical person, when your friend says something the first time, you might not entirely believe him. But, let's say that you check it out and find out that it's true. He says something a second time, you check it out, and it's true. If this keeps happening every time for a thousand times, you find out that this friend has a perfect record for truthfulness. Whenever you check out his story, he's always correct. Always. We call this "credibility."

Credibility wins you some very big points in a courtroom. As a lawyer, I like to have credible witnesses. The Bible is a credible witness. So, on the thousand and first time that the friend tells you something, and you realize that this time you don't have proof (or the time) to check whether he's right or wrong, what do you do? Do you doubt him? No! You believe him! You accept the testimony. That's exactly how the Bible works. You believe based on its credibility—its "track record." And that's how faith works.

Sure, we take some of this stuff on faith, but it's not a "blind leap of faith in the dark," as some might claim. In every place where the Bible can be verified, it proves true. It stands tall. Where it cannot be verified, we should believe it because it has credibility. It has earned it. That's how a trial lawyer and evidence experts treat a credible witness. Sometimes, an entire case stands on a single credible witness. The Bible is that witness.

> **You believe based on its credibility—its "track record."**

EXHIBIT D

THE BIBLE CONTAINS A LIFE-CHANGING MESSAGE OF INDIVIDUAL FREEDOM

"Do not conform to the pattern of this world, but be transformed by the renewing of your mind. Then you will be able to test and approve what God's will is—his good, pleasing and perfect will."

—Romans 12:2

Unlike any other holy book, the Bible has never been in the custody of one single individual or group. Unlike the Qur'an (which was more or less controlled by one group, all male), the Bible, belongs to everybody and nobody at the same time. As we have seen, the Bible has been subjected to scholarly criticism like no other book in history. By contrast, Muslims are not allowed to critique or challenge the Qur'an.

Unlike any other holy book, the Bible has never been in the custody of one single individual or group.

That, alone, should tell us a lot about the Bible's importance. It stands up to criticism. It is God's message to humankind. That message was designed to change us. It's spiritual nourishment to our souls.

The Bible tells us to "taste and see that the Lord is good."[1] We are all individually supposed to test the Word of God. You may know nothing about God, or you may think you know everything about God, but you never really know anything about God unless you read the Bible. "Try it," we're told. See if it works. When you do, you discover that it does. God will change your life for the better! Take the challenge.

What would you pay to spend a half hour interviewing God? Here's a secret: an interview with God and reading the Bible will tell you the same exact thing. Yet, so many of us have Bibles sitting on our shelves that we simply don't read. The Bible is God's revelation of Himself in word and deed to humanity. The Bible has a life-changing message of freedom from bondage, and we need to read it.

FROM HUNTER TO HUNTED

It would probably be fitting to begin this section with one of the first-recorded instances in history where the facts recorded in the Bible made a 180-degree change in someone's life: the Apostle Paul. Born Saul of Tarsus in the early 1st Century, he was a Roman citizen by birth. Trained as a Pharisee, one of the teachers of the Jewish law, Paul was an intellectual of the first rank. He was a believer in all the Jewish scriptures and was trained in them thoroughly under the influential first century Jewish rabbi, Gamaliel. Although we can't be certain of this, most scholars believe it likely that Paul was a member of the Sanhedrin, the Jewish High Court, because of New Testament references in which it is mentioned that Paul had the authority to cast a vote to put someone to death for violations of Jewish law.[2] But, whether Paul was a member of the Sanhedrin or not, he clearly was an important first century Jewish scholar, lawyer, and figure.[3]

In one of his later letters, he says, "For you have heard of my previous way of life in Judaism, how intensely I persecuted the church of God and tried to destroy it. I was advancing in Judaism beyond many of my own age among my people and was extremely zealous for the traditions of my fathers."[4] Clearly Paul was an ambitious Jewish legal scholar, well-versed in Jewish law and the Scriptures. What Paul is referring to in these verses is his zealous commitment as a law-loving, law-abiding Jewish lawyer, sold out to the law of Moses as laid out in the Torah and the remainder of the Tanakh. Paul is saying, in effect, by referring to his training, "I know this stuff better than anybody, so I have a right to discuss this with authority." And he did have every right to.

What is also certain is that Paul was a violent opponent of Christianity, which in its early days was referred to as "The Way." This is probably in reference to Jesus' own words recorded in John 14:6 where He says "I am the way and the truth and the life. No one comes to the Father except through me." Jesus preached about "the way" to God being only through Himself. Paul, as a Jewish prosecutor, was hell-bent on destroying that idea. To Paul, it was criminal to accept the idea of Jesus as anything but a fraud, an impostor, and a false Messiah.

All who believed it must be put in prison, according to Paul. To Paul, God could not be a man."

In Acts, Chapter 7, Paul was present at the death of Stephen (the first martyr, as stated in verse 58). While the crowd was stoning Stephen, the witnesses laid their coats at the feet of a "young man named Saul" (a reference to Saul of Tarsis who was later referred to as "Paul, the Apostle"). Stephen was a righteous man of God who was proclaiming Jesus of Nazareth as the Messiah in fulfillment of the Jewish scriptures. Paul was fully in favor of putting him to death. He was a willing participant, if not the ringleader and agitator of this execution. As recorded in Acts 22:20, here are the very words Paul uttered in confession during a court proceeding: "...and when the blood of... [the] martyr Stephen was shed, I stood there giving my approval and guarding the clothes of those who were killing him."

So, Paul was a violent opponent of Christianity, and the idea of Jews believing in Jesus as the Messiah in fulfillment of their Scriptures made him very angry. So angry, that he actively sought out letters of authority from the High Priest and the religious leaders in Jerusalem to travel to Jewish communities in other cities to persecute the followers of Jesus in those places.[5]

Paul was a violent, murderous persecutor and tormentor of the followers of Jesus. His persecutions also involved dragging off innocent women whose only "crime" was to accept Jesus as the fulfillment of the Jewish Scriptures. Instead of merely arguing against the claim, as civilized people do today (hopefully), Paul advocated using violence to snuff out early Christianity. As recorded in Acts 8:3: "[b]ut Saul began to destroy the church. Going from house to house, he dragged off both men and women and put them in prison." He wreaked havoc, heaping torment upon the early Christians in the name of "religion." Paul is later recorded as saying during his trial testimony:

> "I too was convinced that I ought to do all that was possible to oppose the name of Jesus of Nazareth. And that is just what I did in Jerusalem. On the authority of the chief priests I put many of the Lord's people in prison; and when they were put to death, I cast my vote against them. Many a time I went from one synagogue to another to have them punished, and I tried to force them to blaspheme. I was so obsessed with persecuting them that I even hunted them down in foreign cities."[6]

Paul's view was that belief in Jesus was enough to warrant putting someone to death. We hope and pray that this doesn't happen again in our civilized world, but it has become increasingly evident that belief in Jesus (Christianity) has come under attack to such an extent that it may again come to this, eventually. Already, in radical Islamic countries, people are being killed for this belief, much as they were in ancient times. Sadly, it is not unusual for people to resort to violence when they run out of arguments and erupt in hatred towards the followers of Jesus and His teachings. This is a sad commentary on humanity, but it is a fact.

But something changed in Paul, and that's the point that must be made here. Overnight, Paul went from being a violent persecutor of Christianity to a man who was willing to be persecuted himself for his faith in Jesus. He willingly went from persecutor to persecuted for this same cause. Paul, one-time murderer, a man who was party to the torments of others for their belief in Jesus, became a man who was willingly put in chains, whipped, beaten, and ultimately executed for his beliefs in this very same Jesus that he initially hated so much.

What accounts for this dramatic change, and how exactly did it happen? The story is the subject of numerous artworks and books and is as famous as it is dramatic. Let's hear Paul tell it in his own words. Again, this is his trial testimony, recorded for posterity:

> "Brothers and fathers, listen now to my defense. When they heard him speak to

them in Aramaic, they became very quiet. Then Paul said: I am a Jew, born in Tarsus of Cilicia, but brought up in this city. I studied under Gamaliel and was thoroughly trained in the law of our ancestors. I was just as zealous for God as any of you are today. I persecuted the followers of this Way [i.e. Christianity] to their death, arresting both men and women and throwing them into prison, as the high priest and all the Council can themselves testify. I even obtained letters from them to their associates in Damascus, and went there to bring these people as prisoners to Jerusalem to be punished.

"About noon as I came near Damascus, suddenly a bright light from heaven flashed around me. I fell to the ground and heard a voice say to me, 'Saul! Saul! Why do you persecute me?' 'Who are you, Lord?', I asked. 'I am Jesus of Nazareth, whom you are persecuting,' he replied. My companions saw the light, but they did not understand the voice of him who was speaking to me. 'What shall I do, Lord?', I asked. 'Get up,' the Lord said, 'and go into

Damascus. There you will be told all that you have been assigned to do.'

"My companions led me by the hand into Damascus, because the brilliance of the light had blinded me. A man named Ananias came to see me. He was a devout observer of the law and highly respected by all the Jews living there. He stood beside me and said, 'Brother Saul, receive your sight!' And at that very moment I was able to see him. Then he said: 'The God of our ancestors has chosen you to know his will and to see the Righteous One and to hear words from his mouth. You will be his witness to all people of what you have seen and heard. And now what are you waiting for? Get up, be baptized, and wash your sins away, calling on his name.' When I returned to Jerusalem and was praying at the temple, I fell into a trance and saw the Lord speaking to me. 'Quick!', he said. 'Leave Jerusalem immediately, because the people here will not accept your testimony about me.' 'Lord," I replied, 'these people know that I went from one synagogue to another to imprison and beat those who believe in you. And when the blood of your martyr Stephen was shed, I stood there giving my approval and guarding the clothes of those who were killing him.' Then the Lord said to me, 'Go; I will send you far away to the Gentiles.'"[7]

The crowd listened to Paul until he said this. Then they raised their voices and shouted, "Rid the earth of him! He's not fit to live!" I imagine they did not like his testimony.

This story represents an unusual turn of events for Saul of Tarsis. He was soon to be known as Paul the Apostle, one of the great leaders of the early Church. Paul went on to write fully two-thirds of the New

> **This story represents an unusual turn of events for Saul of Tarsis. He was soon to be known as Paul the Apostle, one of the great leaders of the early Church.**

Testament. Now associated mostly with Christianity, many often forget how he started as a violent man who utterly hated Christians.

Obviously, Paul was a person who didn't do things in a half-hearted manner, and this was likely the reason that God chose him to do this work. God had to know that Paul was "all in" whenever he was involved in doing something in which he believed strongly. It was part of his personality and makeup to be zealous for his beliefs.

But to switch sides from one ideology to the complete opposite in the middle of an ideological and religious "war" is unheard of—unless something unusual truly did happen.

Paul's story has all the hallmarks of truth because his conversion makes utterly no sense without the supernatural component to which he continuously testifies. Nobody fully persuaded to a position will change to the complete opposite viewpoint unless something dramatic happens to cause that change. Earlier, we discussed the conversion of James, the half-brother of Jesus. It takes something dramatic to cause this. This is an example of the life-changing power of the Bible. The Bible refers to this radical change in the core of one's being as being "born again."[8]

The disciples of Christ were transformed from ordinary people to powerful men and women of leadership. They were fisherman, tax collectors, and other "regular folk" before being handpicked by Jesus. But they witnessed some amazing things. Three of Jesus' closest disciples had the privilege of witnessing His transformation into a glorious supernatural being on the so-called "Mount of Transfiguration." This experience left quite a mark on them as they heard and saw things completely from another world. Simon Peter, particularly, was apparently so overwhelmed by this experience that he became somewhat of a blubbering idiot, temporarily uttering nonsense (as recorded in the Gospels).[9]

This experience prompted him to write in his epistle to the Church that "[w]e are not followers of cleverly invented fables, but we were eyewitnesses of his majesty."[10] These are the very same men who penned accounts of their time with Jesus. As John writes, "These things are written that you might believe and that by believing you might have life in his name."[11] What is John talking about? Previously, Jesus was giving a particularly hard teaching, and some of those listening were not able to bear it and they left. Jesus turned to His disciples and asked, "Would you like to leave also?" Peter responded by saying "Where would we go? You have the words of eternal life."[12] He was right. He stuck around, as did many others who had been similarly transformed.

TRANFORMING SOCIETY, ONE PERSON AT A TIME

The Bible not only transforms individuals, it transforms societies. Women were considered to be merely property in the first century. They were not educated and they were not allowed to talk in synagogues.[13] First-century societies, Hebrew and Roman, disregarded women. That's how some religions treat women in modern times. Go to Saudi Arabia and see how women are treated there. However, this is not the way the Bible treats women. The Bible exalts women and honors womanhood. I get upset when people say, "The Bible tries to keep women down." That's nonsense. The role of women is honored in the Bible. Remember, women were the first witnesses to the Resurrection!

God very clearly teaches that we are all created in His image and likeness. God has both female and male qualities because He is a sexless being (even though Jesus, God in human flesh, is male). The Bible is very clear that "in Christ, there is no male, no female; no slave, no free; no Jew, no Gentile."[14] This was a shocking thing to say in the ancient world. It was another revolutionary concept recorded in the Bible. It transformed relations between men and women. The Bible removes the barriers of gender, race, position, and wealth that societies erect. There is no racism, feminism, segregation, prejudice, or class distinctions in Christ. The Bible teaches this.

The Romans were really puzzled by this whole "Christianity thing." The Romans had a lot of societies, groups that would gather for different purposes. The Romans were no strangers to the idea of organizations that were not governmental. Today we would use the term "not for profit" organizations, and in some countries they are called "NGOs" (non-governmental organizations). What really puzzled them was that in every Roman organization, senators socialized with other senators, slaves socialized with slaves, plebeians socialized with plebeians, and so on. They never mixed across social or sexual lines (usually). The social lines of status were clearly defined and rarely crossed. Christianity changed all of that. The Bible changed society.

FROM SINNER TO SAINT

The Bible can also change one's character. Throughout history, there are many examples of the Bible influencing "the captives" and setting them free. One great example is found in the life of St. Augustine of Hippo. St. Augustine was born in 354 AD to a devout Christian mother and a pagan father. Augustine's youth was described as "loose living," a constant search for answers to life's basic questions.[15] Instead of searching the Bible for these answers, Augustine put his trust in the teachings of philosophers, only to grow dissatisfied with their explanations. He was "captive" to bad ideas and to his own passions. He lived a wild and dissolute life. He was a lust-driven, womanizing, carousing man.[16]

In the year 386, Augustine was spending some time in Milan. He recounted that he passed by a child singing, "Pick it up and read it. Pick it up read it," which he took as a divine command from God to open the Bible and read the first thing he saw. The first passage he turned to was Romans 13:13–14, instructing, "Let us behave decently, as in the daytime, not in carousing and drunkenness, not in sexual immorality and debauchery, not in dissension and jealousy. Rather, clothe yourselves with the Lord Jesus Christ, and do not think about how to gratify the desires of the flesh." Reading this Scripture, Augustine was filled with the Spirit and turned away from his sinful life.[17] He went on to become a great theologian of the Church, and his life and writings eventually earned him the title of "Saint" Augustine.

AMAZING GRACE

Another life that once was "blind" and learned to "see" by the Scriptures was that of John Newton. Newton is the author of one of the most famous Christian hymns in history: "Amazing Grace." You might be surprised to learn that this hymn was not written by someone who spent his entire life as a believer, grew up in the Church, and always recognized Jesus as his Savior. In fact, John Newton actually spent a portion of his life as a slave trader!

Like many people, Newton was exposed to the Gospel by his mother at a very early age. His mother taught him to read Scripture and memorize hymns, and the two would always attend church together each week in London.[18] This routine was not present in Newton's life for very long. His mother passed away when he was only seven years old, leaving him in the care of his less religious (and more distant) father.[19] In his father's care, Newton received seafaring lessons, and, under the lenient hand of his stepmother, he was allowed to roam free and get himself into all kinds of youthful troubles.[20] Although he fell into temptation time and time again, Newton repeatedly would try to turn back to the Christian teachings his mother imparted on him.[21]

Newton's life saw a spiritual pivot in 1748 when he was 23 years old. During a sea voyage, his ship was caught in a terrible storm for well over a week.[22] In the midst of this terrifying storm, Newton began to reflect on how disconnected his life had become from God. He had rejected his mother's teachings and even led fellow sailors to unbelief.[23]

> Newton's life saw a spiritual pivot in 1748 when he was 23 years old. During a sea voyage, his ship was caught in a terrible storm for well over a week.

He found hope when he picked up a copy of the New Testament and read the words of Luke 11:13—"If you then, though you are evil, know how to give good gifts to your children, how much more will your Father in heaven give the Holy Spirit to those who ask him!"

Although he continued his profession of sailing and slave trading for some time after, Newton's life was transformed as he began to discipline himself in the study of the Gospel and set a Christian example for his fellow sailors.[24] Newton's Christian devotions inspired him to leave the slave trade and eventually pursue a life in ministry. Newton led Thursday night prayer services in his home and often wrote a hymn to be sung at each service to a familiar tune.[25] "Amazing Grace" was likely one of these hymns that Newton wrote for his prayer services sometime between 1760 and 1770.[26] The origin of the melody is unknown, but many speculate that Newton applied his words to the tune of a song sung by slaves.[27]

REFLECTIONS ON THE PEANUT

Even a life well-lived can be enhanced by the power of Scripture. The Bible motivates and enables anyone who seeks its wisdom and uses it as intended, to get closer to God and to discover your life's purpose. All our lives have a purpose.

For life to have purpose, it must have meaning. What is your purpose in life? It's amazing to me that so few people even know the answer to this question about their own existence. People used to ask these hard questions of themselves (I call them "THE BIG QUESTIONS"), but it seems that nowadays, this type of self-introspection has been drowned out by televisions, the Internet, and iPods (toys, in other words). Let me tell you about a man who took the purpose of his life very seriously.

The South had been hit by agricultural disaster in the early 1900s on account of a depletion in the soil caused by over-planting and excessive reliance on cotton as the chief agricultural crop of southern farmers. Land that used to be much more productive was now yielding a fraction of what it had once produced. The result was certain economic disaster unless a solution could be found.

Enter George Washington Carver, a son of slaves. After his mother had been captured and sold off, never to be seen again, George was raised by a Christian family as one of their own. This brilliant young man had a natural curiosity and a thirst for knowledge that was uncanny. He was truly one of the most remarkable men of all time. We usually hear about his creative genius, but he was gifted in music, science, art, and many academic areas. What's not often emphasized about him, though, is his deep faith in an almighty creator God who, if asked, might unlock the secrets of the Universe to anyone who sincerely approached Him and asked for His guidance.

In response to the plight of the southern economy and the resulting poverty and economic hardship, George got on his knees in prayer. It's reported that young George Washington Carver asked God (in a prayer) to unlock the secrets of creation to him, but God responded by saying, "It's too much for your puny mind." George then limited his request to agriculture in general, but received the same response: "It's still too much for your brain to handle." After a bit of meditation and prayer, George finally asked God to help him unlock the secrets of the peanut. Allegedly, God responded in the affirmative.

The rest is history. The following is excerpted from one of many histories of George Washington Carver's life readily available on the internet:

"Cotton had long been the South's primary agricultural crop. But planting cotton decade after decade, without rotating crops, depleted the soil. Mounting debts plagued farmers. George urged farmers to reinvigorate their soil by planting peanuts and sweet potatoes. After some persuasion, farmers made peanuts and sweet potatoes number one in the South by devoting more and more acreage to these crops.

The problem was that no real markets existed for peanuts or sweet potatoes. No one wanted to buy the product, so it rotted in the fields, and farmers lost even more money. This disaster nearly crushed George. Deeply concerned, he prayed to God, 'Mr. Creator, why did you make the peanut?'"

George later wrote that God led him back to his laboratory. There, through hard work and persistence, he discovered some 300 valuable products that could be made—and marketed—from the peanut. Among them were cooking oil, mayonnaise, cheese, shampoo, instant coffee, flour, soap, face powder, plastics, adhesives, axle grease, and pickles.

From the sweet potato, Carver derived more than 100 products such as starch, library paste, vinegar, shoe polish, ink, and molasses. The demand for peanuts and sweet potatoes soared. Economists and agriculturalists agree: George Washington Carver did more than any other person to revive the South's economy.

When he died in 1943, Carver's epitaph read, "He could have added fortune to fame, but caring for neither, he found happiness and honor in being helpful to the world."

Mr. Carver was honored for his life and contributions by the President, political leaders, and the major business leaders of his day, including Henry Ford. He was a remarkable man, all because of a simple prayer and a humble desire to help others. God is a God of Science. He created all things, and therefore, understands how all things operate. Sometimes, he allows us to peer into the secrets if we ask humbly and with good motives.

RUN, BABY, RUN!

In 1958, a Pennsylvania country preacher named David Wilkerson found himself in New York City attempting to speak with seven young gang members who were on trial for murder. Seeing the tragic effects of drug abuse on these people, Wilkerson soon founded "Teen

Challenge," a program to reach gang members with a message of God's love.[28] The purpose of the program was to create a space to take in drug-addicted gang members and teach them how to live as drug-free Christians in the real world.[29] That message of God's love and forgiveness has allowed "Teen Challenge" to spread, and today it helps over 28,000 men, women, boys, and girls who face life-controlling problems.

According to his autobiography, *Run Baby Run*, Nicky Cruz was a violent member of a Puerto Rican gang (the "MauMaus") in New York City in the early 1960s. When he first heard the message of the Gospel of Jesus Christ from Pastor David Wilkerson, he responded by threatening to kill him. Angry and violent, Cruz's own mother referred to him as "son of Satan." When he finally converted to Christianity by repenting of his sins and accepting the message and

> It's amazing to see God's power to change lives in action through programs like "Teen Challenge."

person of Jesus Christ, his life was radically transformed. Nicky began studying the Bible and ultimately became a preacher, ministering on the streets to gang members. His story was made into a major motion picture starring Pat Boone (as Rev. Wilkerson), *The Cross and the Switchblade* (1970).[30] He is still in ministry today, over five decades later.

It's amazing to see God's power to change lives in action through programs like "Teen Challenge." There have also been empirical studies that show that "faith-based programs" are more effective in enabling people to overcome addiction and illness. A study of New York inmates who participated in their prison Bible studies showed them to have a much lower rate of relapse when compared with a group of inmates who did not attend the Bible studies.[31] Regarding Teen Challenge's drug treatment program, specifically, a Public Health Service study found it to be more effective than its secular counterparts.[32] The Bible sets people free from substance abuse because it changes people.

FREEDOM FROM THE BONDAGE OF RELIGION

An even more modern example of the Bible being a roadmap to freedom can be found in the testimony of Nabeel Qureshi. Nabeel was born in the United States and was raised by devout Muslim parents who were Pakistani immigrants. From a very early age, Nabeel was taught Muslim prayers and practices, and he held these teachings close to his heart.[33] His family was from a priestly tribe believed to be descended from the same tribe as Mohammed.

In 2001, as a freshman in college, Nabeel made friends with a Christian, David Wood. Nabeel decided to question David on his knowledge of the Bible, and particularly, its legitimacy. Nabeel's questions focused largely on whether the text of the Bible had been corrupted throughout history. One such question was, "Why are there constantly so many new editions and revisions of the Bible?" Nabeel believed that Christ never claimed to be God, and that Christians had manipulated the Scriptures throughout history to "create" such a claim.[34] This is a typical Muslim belief about Christians and the New Testament.

Before I go any further with this story, don't you feel as though we've seen enough evidence so far to counter Nabeel's way of thinking? Here's how David responded:

- There is such a large amount of early manuscript evidence and so much agreement between those manuscripts that we can reconstruct the Bible and be certain of about 95% of the original content (a conservative estimate, when in actuality it's closer to 98 or 99%).
- No doctrine of the Bible is in jeopardy from any of the textual variations.
- There are so many quotations of and references to the New Testament from the ancient world that we can reconstruct practically all of it from early quotations alone.

- There are multiple fragments of manuscripts that can be dated to within a couple of centuries after Christ's death which we have in our possession even now.

- Entire copies of the Bible are available from around three centuries after Christ's death.[35]

This was enough evidence for Nabeel, a devout Muslim, to want to dig deeper into the Christian faith and question his previously-held beliefs on the authenticity of biblical Scripture. Nabeel began to study the Scripture and saw for himself that everything David had said was true. Applying the same sort of in-depth historical analysis to his Islamic faith, Nabeel was unable to replicate a similar result. Tormented by this realization and feeling as if he had nowhere left to go, Nabeel opened up the New Testament and was quickly drawn in, coming to the realization that the Bible had revealed to him the identity of the most important person in history.[36] Nabeel gave up everything his life was founded on to follow Jesus. I have had both David Wood and Nabeel Qureshi in my law office as clients and friends and can personally attest to their story, although sadly, Nabeel is no longer with us, having recently passed on.

Transformations of people from the truths found in the Bible continue to this very day. The Bible records the words of God which are able to transform people into what God intended them to be. "Be not conformed to this world: but be ye transformed by the renewing of your mind" (Romans 12:2 (KJV)).

According to Michael J. Kruger:

"One example [of the divine quality of the Bible] is the efficacy and power of Scripture. It's not just that Scripture says things, but the Scripture does things. It convicts (Heb. 4:12–13), it encourages (Ps. 119:105), it comforts (v. 50), and it brings wisdom (v. 98). In short, this book is alive. Even more than this, the Bible brings understanding in regard to the biggest questions of life (v. 144). It provides a coherent and compelling worldview that explains reality like no other book."[37]

The Bible transforms lives because it is the very Word of God, and there is power in the Word of God.

EXHIBIT E

AN INTRODUCTION TO THE MOST IMPORTANT PERSON IN HISTORY

"I am the way and the truth and the life. No one comes to the Father except through me."

—John 14:6

The most important reason the Bible is the most important book ever written is that it introduces us to the most important person in history: Jesus Christ, the god-man.

Jesus of Nazareth is, without doubt, the most famous person who has ever lived. There is barely anyone in the entire world who hasn't heard of him. People name their children after him. He is believed to be a prophet of God by fully two-thirds of the people in the world (Christians and Muslims). He is truly the most important person who has ever lived. This can hardly be disputed.

If you know nothing about Jesus of Nazareth, you will quickly find out all you need to know by reading the Bible. I always

> **Jesus of Nazareth is, without doubt, the most famous person who has ever lived.**

get a kick out of critics on TV who say things about Jesus—you quickly realize that they've probably never read the Bible, since most of what they say is contradicted by it. Their opinions are highly questionable, but it makes for some interesting television!

As a prime example, the "Jesus Seminar" in the '80s was a group of skeptics (they called themselves "scholars") sitting around and "venting" their opinions about the Bible. Their method of truth verification was to cast votes for the probability of Jesus' various claims. How is a seminar that votes on facts concerning Jesus remotely academic? It's weird, prideful, and delusional. And why follow someone else's opinion about Jesus when the facts are recorded in the Bible, allowing you to make your own decision? What matters here are facts, not **opinions.**

Opinions are based on feelings and conclusions while facts are objective realities that stand on their own.

Everybody has an opinion about Jesus. When you press some people about those opinions, you can quickly find out that many have not even read the New Testament, the primary source about Jesus. In 384 AD, Saint Jerome, the man who translated the Vulgate at the request of the Pope, said "[t]o know Scripture is to know Christ, to not know Scripture is to not know Christ."[1] And he's right! You can't know anything significant about Jesus if you don't know the New Testament. Having an opinion about Jesus without ever reading the New Testament is like having an opinion about Shakespeare without ever having read any of his plays.

> Opinions are based on feelings and conclusions while facts are objective realities that stand on their own.

There was an article in a recent edition of *Decision Magazine* which points out how biblically ignorant many Christians are today.[2] No one is reading the Bible, so they don't know what to believe about Jesus, God, or Christian practice. Without the Bible, all we have is blind faith in a person, Jesus, who we don't really know. This is dangerous, because then we can "invent" a Christ of our own design. But that's only wishful thinking and self-deception. Jesus is a real person with words that can be accurately ascertained. Otherwise, Christianity would be a fraud.

It's impossible to be indifferent about Jesus Christ. You either love Jesus or you hate Him. I think C.S. Lewis put it best when he said:

> "I am trying here to prevent anyone saying the really foolish thing that people often say about Him: I'm ready to accept Jesus as a great moral teacher, but I do not accept his claim to be God. That is the one thing we must not say. A man who was merely a man and said the sort of things Jesus said would not be a great moral teacher. He would either be a lunatic—on the level with the man who says he is a poached egg—or else he would be the Devil of Hell. You must make your choice. Either this man was, and

is, the Son of God, or else a madman or something worse. You can shut him up for a fool, you can spit at him and kill him as a demon or you can fall at his feet and call him Lord and God, but let us not come with any patronizing nonsense about his being a great human teacher. He has not left that open to us. He did not intend to... Now it seems to me obvious that He was neither a lunatic nor a fiend: and consequently, however strange or terrifying or unlikely it may seem, I have to accept the view that He was and is God."[3]

So, Jesus is either Lord, lunatic, or liar. It's impossible to get away with saying "Jesus was a good teacher, but I don't believe he was God in human form." As C.S. Lewis says, that option is not available to us. Jesus is either everything He said He was, or He is nothing He said He was. He is either God, or He's a fraud or a mental case. He has to be God in human form. There is really no other legitimate option. Nobody could do or say the things that Jesus did and said unless they were truly someone very extraordinary.

The Bible is the same way. As we saw, the Bible claims to be the Word of God over 2,000 times. It's either the biggest fraud ever perpetrated on mankind, or it's everything it claims to be. It simply cannot be any other way. The Bible records the very words of God. There's no middle ground. It's either the Word of God, or it's not. Every person must decide whether they believe it to be the truth. I have come to a decision on what to believe. I have no problem believing the Bible is everything it says it is and that Jesus is everything he claimed to be. The Bible records the truth about God and about Jesus, and the evidence supports that.

JESUS CLAIMED TO BE GOD

If you read Dan Brown's *The Da Vinci Code*, you may get the impression that Jesus was just a wise teacher who came teaching us a higher morality. You may also get the impression that Jesus never claimed to be God. According to Leagh Teabing, a character in the book, Jesus was voted into Godhood in 325 AD at the Council of Nicea at the urging of the Roman Emperor Constantine. That is an outright fabrication, yet most people accept it because most people have very little knowledge of historical facts. People who know little of history try to make the claim that Jesus "evolved" over time into a "godlike" figure. It's simply not true.

Jesus Christ did not "evolve" into God status. He was always God and He has always claimed to be God. His disciples and others understood this. Christ was even acknowledged to be believed by Christians to be God in ancient Roman writings. Pliny knew this as early as 100 AD when he wrote to the Emperor Trajan. He said the Christians "used to gather on a stated day before dawn and sing to Christ as if he were a god, and they took an oath not to involve themselves in villainy, but rather to commit no theft, no fraud, no adultery; not to break faith, nor to deny money placed with them in trust. Once these things were done, it was their custom to part and return later to eat a meal together…"[4] Even the pagan Romans knew that Jesus claimed to be God from the time He first began his ministry. It was no secret.

Indeed, there was a vote at the Council of Nicaea, but that vote was not over whether Jesus is God or not. The issue actually was this: "what kind of God is Jesus?" That's an important difference. The Romans had more or less copied the Greek culture, so they believed in many gods just as the Greeks did. They had no problem believing that Jesus was God (the Gentiles, at least, even if the Jews had a hard time with it). As Gentiles began to make up more of the Church—as it became more "Greek" and less Jewish—the issue arose from Arias and his followers: is Jesus co-eternal, co-equal, and of the same type and substance as the Father? This was the issue at the Council of Nicaea. The Council met to consider whether Jesus was God in the same way as God the Father, not whether

He is God. Nobody at that council doubted that Jesus was "God."

In *The Da Vinci Code*, Dan Brown also says that it was a "close vote" at the Council of Nicaea. Maybe it was if you consider 316 to 3 a close vote. Perhaps Brown meant to say "close to unanimous." The only dissenters were Arias and his two followers, and they left the Council branded as heretics. They refused to recant their positions, but even they believed Jesus was "a God." They just took the position that Jesus was less than the Father God. This is all recorded with great specificity by Eusebius (Eusebius of Caesarea was a Bishop, a scholar, and an important historian), the official "minute keeper" of Emperor Constantine.

The whole point is that Jesus was believed by His followers to be God way before the Council of Nicaea. The disciples believed that Jesus was God even when Jesus walked the earth with them. It was not a concept that developed later with time. It was the thinking right from the beginning. It was this claim—Jesus being God—that got Jesus in trouble with the authorities. Jesus never officially uttered the words (as far as we know) "I am God," but he said it in so many other ways that it's too lengthy to list them here. This was from the days of His ministry. It was not a later legend that evolved.

Jesus said that the Scriptures "are they which testify of me."[5] He was referring to the Jewish Bible in use there at the time, which was called the Septuagint. The Septuagint was a Greek translation of the Jewish Bible (the Tanakh). The Jews believed (and still do) that the Tanakh is Scripture, the Word of God. Jesus claimed that the Tanakh, in reality, was really all about Him. That is quite a claim, and it's tantamount to saying "I am God." That, plus many other statements by Jesus, clearly indicate that he claimed to be God right from the start.

It must have taken a lot for Jesus to convince his Jewish, monotheistic brother to believe that he was God! Scholars believe that James' change of heart was primarily due to seeing his brother Jesus risen from the dead after being crucified. That's what it would take for most people to accept that their older brother was God in human form. It's mind boggling!

Since Jews were the earliest followers of Jesus, first-century Judaism was harshly divided on the issue. Was Jesus God? Was he the Messiah (Hebrew for "Anointed One")? Was he the Christ (Greek for "Messiah")? Was Jesus an imposter? The Bible, in its entirety, answers this question. In fact, it is the question that everyone needs to answer, and the clues are in the Bible. But, you can't even attempt to answer this question if you don't know the Bible.

The Jewish Bible foretold that a great deliverer would come at a future date. This was predictive prophecy foretold years—even centuries—in advance of the fulfillment. In one famous passage, the Jewish prophet Isaiah writes, "His name shall be called wonderful, counselor, the mighty God, the Everlasting Father, the Prince of Peace."[6] This passage—widely accepted by Jews as "Messianic," meaning it referred to the future Messiah—clearly describes the Messiah figure as "God." How else can this be interpreted? Therefore, the Jewish Bible clearly foretold of a Messiah who would be God. Yet other prophetic passages refer to the Messiah as a man. Was there a mix-up here? A problem with interpretation? Two opposing views? Or was it possible that the long-awaited Messiah would be both man and God in human form? Christian theology teaches that Jesus

> **The miracles performed were not disputed. The only dispute was over the power behind them.**

was both God and man, having two natures. He was God incarnate in human form (exactly as he appeared at times in the Torah).

When Jesus walked the earth, he dazzled the multitudes with great miracles. His detractors, mostly the Jewish elite, did not deny these miracles but, rather, attributed them to witchcraft, sorcery, or "the power of the devil."[7] Others said "this man has to be from God" because of these great works.[8] The miracles performed were not disputed. The only dispute was over the power behind them.

In fact, the Talmud records an early traditional Jewish teaching which corroborates the New Testament record of how the Jewish leaders viewed the claims of Jesus. In a disputed passage (which, due to "political correctness" was attempted to be censored out) it states as follows:

"It was taught: On the Eve of Passover they hung Yeshua the Notzarine [Jesus the Nazarene]. And the herald went out before him for 40 days [saying]: 'Yeshua the Notzarine will go out to be stoned for sorcery and misleading and enticing Israel [to idolatry]. Any who knows [anything] in his defense must come and declare concerning him.' But no-one came to his defense, so they hung him on the Eve of Passover."

Clearly, this accurately records the Jewish leaders' rejection of Christ's miracles as "sorcery" and does not dispute them. It constitutes corroboration from a hostile source that seeks to attribute his power to evil and not to God. Amazingly, this is exactly what the New Testament records actually happened. Jesus' miracles were not denied (they could not deny them) but were attributed to Satan! In Luke 11:14–15, "Jesus was driving out a demon...When the demon left, the man who had been mute spoke, and the crowd was amazed. But some of them said, 'By Beelzebub [the devil], the prince of demons, he is driving out demons.' Clearly, the earliest Jewish rejection of Jesus was based on WHERE he derived his power from, not WHETHER he had it.

Because Jesus claimed to be God and demonstrated it with miracles, the first-century Jews were divided on the question of Jesus. Jewish people are fiercely monotheistic: they hold firmly to the belief in only one God. The lynchpin of Jewish belief is a liturgical prayer called the Shema, which states: "Hear O Israel, the Lord your God is one God..."[9] Thus, Jesus' claim to be God in human form caused quite an uproar in the Jewish community. But Jesus never claimed to be a "second God." Jesus is better understood as God in human form. He was the perfect revelation of God so that we could grasp God for ourselves. He was the physical manifestation of God, according to the New Testament. That simply didn't sit well with some people.

Some Jews did accept Jesus as God. They believed His claims, because they saw the miracles and they witnessed His resurrection. They also saw his compassion for the sick and the poor, something that does not equate with "evil." After Jesus' resurrection, these Jews became gradually known as Christians. Over time, the followers of Jesus became less and less Jewish, especially as Gentiles became followers of Christ, adding to their numbers. Eventually, the followers of Christ (i.e. "the Church") lost their Jewish flavor almost entirely. This is a pretty sad, yet historically accurate, fact. With the exception of the Old Testament, the Church now retains almost nothing of its Jewish roots. This is unfortunate, not only because of the

Jewishness of Jesus, but also because Christianity cannot be understood properly without a Jewish context. You really need a Jewish context to fully grasp who Jesus was and who he claimed to be.

Those who remained Jews came to form a belief that Jesus was an imposter, a fraudulent deceiver who claimed to be the Messiah; He was either a madman or an intentional liar. In recent times, Jews have softened their stance on Jesus by granting Him status as a "wise man" and a great benevolent teacher (but not God). This is part of the modern effort by people in general to try to be sensitive to the religions of others. But if you really examine this closely, it makes little sense and is utterly inconsistent with recorded history. As C.S. Lewis said, Jesus did not leave us with that option.

So, what did Jesus claim about himself? Let's examine some of these claims so that you can make an informed decision. What evidence is there for Jesus' claim to be God? Is it more probable than not? Is it enough to stake your life on? What's the best explanation for the evidence we have?

For the most part, the common Jewish man of Judea in the first century readily accepted Jesus and His claims. Is this because he was gullible and ignorant? Or, is this because he had no vested interest in the status quo? The powerful ruling body known as the Sanhedrin mostly rejected Jesus' claims (although some did accept them).

They knew that Jesus claimed to be God. They charged Him with blasphemy, saying, "because you, a mere man, make yourself out to be God."[10] Were they correct in their judgment, or did they have a vested interest in the status quo because they were in positions of power and authority and, if Jesus was God, had a lot to lose? These are important questions that bear on the issue of credibility regarding these early witnesses. It's also important to note that some of the powerful elite actually did accept Jesus' claims.

Did Jesus ever actually utter the words "I am God"? He believed he was God and said he was God in many different ways. Jesus said, "All power in heaven and earth is given to me."[11] That certainly is a claim to be God. There was no doubt about what Jesus claimed, and Jesus was executed on the charge of blasphemy for claiming to be God! It was obvious what he claimed.

Jesus appeared as a man in order that we might understand Him. My guess is that, if He had appeared as "Sovereign God" we would never have the ability to comprehend Him and would have fallen on our faces cowering in front of His spectacular brilliance. So, He came as a man. As a humble, poor, first-century human being in a world twisted and fallen by hate, wars, crimes, greed, lust, pride, and all manner of general ugliness and brokenness. He did not create it that way, but that's what it had become due to mankind's continual quest for (each of us) getting his own way. The inevitable conflicts that ensued (over property, land, women, men, position, and power) resulted in what was created to be perfect falling into general disorder and chaos. Sure, there were (and still are) vestiges of beauty, but the general order originally created was tending toward chaos, disorder, ugliness, blight, and disaster. Scientists and mathematicians call this "chaos theory" or "the law of entropy." Theologians call this "The Fall," referring to mankind's fall from perfection once we all decided to do things our own way instead of God's way. Regardless of what you label it, the world is tending towards disorder (chaos) and is spinning even more into confusion and brokenness.

Some believe that Jesus cannot be God because God is invisible, and somewhere "out there," and therefore he cannot be present in time and space. Some believe that it would be weird to accept that Jesus is God, because somehow that would be idolatry. Also, they say, it would mean that there are two Gods and that couldn't be possible. How could there be two supremely powerful beings, each called God? Would they cancel the other's power? Who would be the boss?

Jesus, as I have said, is God in human form. He is a separate person, but He is primarily a revelation of God to us in a way that we can grasp. Christians would never say that we worship two Gods. We would simply say that there is one God and He relates to us (reveals Himself to us) in the person of Jesus Christ. Jesus is the ultimate revelation of God to human beings.

Jesus came to earth with a specific purpose and mission in mind. That purpose and mission could not be accomplished unless He was also fully human. He had to be both fully human and fully God to accomplish this mission. That may sound like a contradiction, but He is God and is able to do as He pleases. Fortunately for us, His plan was a good one. You see, God came to earth for the main reason of benefitting us. He came for your benefit and mine. This was a free gift to us and it cost Him a lot. He came to offer Himself as a sacrifice for our sins, to pay the price that we owed, so that we could walk free. He came to die in our place.

Jesus' favorite designation for Himself was "the Son of Man." He referred to himself as "the Son of Man" eighty times in the New Testament. These statements, on the surface, would appear to be stressing Jesus' humanity and not His divinity. The exact opposite is the case. The phrase "Son of Man" was a clear reference to Daniel 7:13 and would have been understood by His first-century, Jewish audience as a clear claim to be God. See here:

"In my vision at night I looked, and there before me was one like a son of man, coming with the clouds of heaven. He approached the Ancient of Days and was led into his presence. He was given authority, glory and sovereign power; all nations and peoples of every language worshiped him. His dominion is an everlasting dominion that will not pass away, and his kingdom is one that will never be destroyed."[12]

In this passage from the Tanakh, we clearly see that worship is given to the "Son of Man" in the presence of God ("the Ancient of Days"), yet God doesn't seem to mind this. Instead, God gives this Son of Man "authority, glory and sovereign power." It sure sounds like the "Son of Man" is God. Furthermore, the kingdom of the "Son of Man" is an "everlasting kingdom that will not pass away." Unless there are two such everlasting kingdoms, this must refer to the Messiah, because David was also promised that one of his bloodline would sit on the throne of Israel forever. Therefore, it's certain then, that this is one and the same Messiah, who is God, is also the "Son of Man." Jesus was calling Himself divine.

The Gospel of Mark is generally accepted as the earliest Gospel to have been written, probably around 50 or 60 AD when many of the witnesses to Christ's ministry were still alive. Mark's Gospel has a close association with the Apostle Peter and it's probable that Mark acted as Peter's scribe since Peter was an uneducated fisherman. Peter had the ability to give a firsthand account of many of Christ's sayings and deeds, but not necessarily the ability to write them down.

In Mark, Chapter 2, there's an interesting account of Jesus at Capernaum. He was preaching before a crowd of people at a home. The Gospel writer records the following:

"They gathered in such large numbers that there was no room left, not even outside the door, and he preached the word to them. Some men came, bringing to him a paralyzed man, carried by four of them. Since they could not get him to Jesus because of the crowd, they made an opening in the roof above Jesus by digging through it and then lowered the mat the man was lying on. When Jesus saw their faith, he said to the paralyzed man, 'Son, your sins are forgiven.'"[13]

Your sins are forgiven? Who makes such a statement, especially in a first century, Jewish context? The significance

> **Your sins are forgiven? Who makes such a statement, especially in a first century, Jewish context?**

of this outrageous comment was certainly not lost on the rabbis sitting there, for their response was one of predictable outrage. "Why does this fellow talk like that? He is blaspheming! Who can forgive sins, but God alone?"[14] Right! This was exactly Jesus' point. He was saying, "I am God." That's why He said it.

And He doesn't stop there. He says, in essence, "For me, it's just as easy to forgive sins as to heal this paralyzed man" [my paraphrase]. Then He says to the paralyzed man, "I tell you, get up, take your mat and go home," at which point the man does exactly that.[15]

To Jews, the Sabbath (Shabbat) is one of the most important aspects of life. It's one of the inviolable Ten Commandments and was sacred beyond description, especially in first-century Palestine. Jesus, in response to the Pharisees' (Jewish religious leaders) charge that he had violated the Sabbath, replied to them, "So the Son of Man [i.e. me] is Lord even of the Sabbath."[16] Astounding! Only God could say that.

In another part of the Gospel of Mark, Jesus was driving out demons. The teachers of the law who came down from Jerusalem said, "He is possessed by Beelzebub! By the prince of demons, he is driving out demons."[17] Notice that these religious leaders did not deny Jesus' power or the wonders that he performed. Their response was not, "What are you talking about? This guy is a fraud! He has no power!" No, they couldn't argue with the obvious miracles and feats they saw with their very own eyes. Their response was that Christ was demon-possessed and derived his power from demons. Jesus' response is classic:

"Every kingdom divided against itself will be laid waste, and every city or household divided against itself will not stand. If Satan drives out Satan, he is divided against himself. How, then, can his kingdom stand?"[18]

This famous answer of Jesus was later to be quoted in part by Abraham Lincoln during the Civil War in his effort to preserve the union of the United States. It remains a powerful truth in every situation.

Jesus was not always understood by those closest to him. After all, who can claim to understand God? We can know some things about God, but God is too vast to be comprehended. Imagine Albert Einstein trying to explain the theory of relativity to an insect; now, multiply that incomprehension by infinity because the gap between us and God is even greater. We can only know such things about God as He chooses to reveal them to us. Consider Christ's own disciples in this story from Mark 4:35–41:

> That day when evening came, he said to his disciples, "Let us go over to the other side." Leaving the crowd behind, they took him along, just as he was, in the boat. There were also other boats with him. A furious squall came up, and the waves broke over the boat, so that it was nearly swamped. Jesus was in the stern, sleeping on a cushion. The disciples woke him and said to him, "Teacher, do not you care if we drown?"
>
> He got up, rebuked the wind and said to the waves, "Quiet! Be still!" Then the wind died down and it was completely calm.

He said to his disciples, "Why are you so
afraid? Do you still have no faith?"

They were terrified and asked each other,
"Who is this? Even the wind and the waves
obey him!"

"Who is this?" Not even Jesus' closest friends were sure
what to make of Him. I mean, He sure must have looked
like a man and Christian theology does teach that Jesus
was also man. They ate with him. They traveled with him.
They talked with him. But He was more than man. He was
God. Who else could speak to nature (Creation) and
command its obedience?

Philip, one of Jesus' disciples, asked Him flat out. He
said, "Lord, show us the Father and that will be enough
for us." Jesus answered and said, "Do not you know me
Philip, even after I have been among you such a long
time? Anyone who has seen me has seen the Father.
How can you say, "Show us the Father?"[19] I'd say that's
a pretty clear answer.

Once, during a lengthy theological debate with
Jewish theologians (too lengthy to be quoted in its
entirety here, but found in John 8:31–59), Jesus was again
accused by his detractors of being "demon-possessed."
Again, they must have seen something pretty scary on a
supernatural level to jump to that conclusion and make

that accusation. Jesus calmly responds: "I tell you the truth... before Abraham was born, I am."[20]

I am! Wow! Jesus used the very words that God used to describe himself to Moses from the burning bush! Even the biblically illiterate have at least seen the movie, *The Ten Commandments*, with Charlton Heston. Moses asked God: "What should I explain to the Israelite nation when I go back to them to announce that I am chosen as their deliverer?" Moses knew the Israelites would rightly question from where Moses got his authority. Who was Moses to

> Who was Moses to tell them who had sent him?

tell them who had sent him? "What is his name? Then what shall I tell them?" Then, "God said to Moses, 'I AM WHO I AM. This is what you are to say to the Israelites: I AM has sent me to you.'"[21]

"I AM" is generally understood to mean "the eternal self-existent one.

" *The one who is and has "being" simply because He is who He is; The Uncaused One, in essence.* Everything has a cause, except God. He is, and only He is the one who always is. That is not bad English! It's just the facts.

Jesus used these words deliberately. Now, even if the biblically ignorant have no idea what Jesus meant, it's certainly clear that Jesus' detractors knew exactly what He said and how He meant it. This could be taken no other way. That is why they "picked up stones to stone him," because this was the method of execution necessary for anyone committing such blasphemy according to the Jewish law.

Further along in the Gospel of John, Jesus gets into another confrontation with the Jewish leaders when He says, "I and the Father are one."[22] At this, they "picked up stones to stone him." Jesus responded by saying (sarcastically) "I have shown you many great miracles from the Father. For which of these do you stone me?" They replied, "We are not stoning you for any of these but for blasphemy, because you, a mere man, claim to be God." Clearly, Jesus claimed to be God. This is not a later legend invented by medieval superstitious people in the Church. It's right there, recorded in the Bible, in the earliest accounts of Jesus. It's also interesting to note that His detractors never denied that He had performed miracles. Those miracles were not in dispute. They were too obvious.

There are many other instances where Jesus claimed to be God in human form. In Matthew 28:18, the resurrected Jesus appears to His disciples, and "when they saw him, they worshiped him." Jesus did not rebuke them for this, but accepted their worship, saying, "All authority in heaven and earth has been given to me." It sure sounds like God talking here. In every other place in the entire Bible, when man worships anything else but God, he is corrected or rebuked.

In John 20:24–28, Thomas (the famous "doubting Thomas") refuses to believe that Jesus has risen from the dead after such a horrible and mutilating death on the cross. Can you really blame him? I mean, people don't usually rise from the dead! He stubbornly claims that he "will not believe it" (v.25) unless he sees and feels for himself the resurrected person of Christ, complete with death scars. Jesus grants his request and appears to Thomas. Stretching out his hands for Thomas to see and touch, Jesus says, in essence, "Go ahead, put your finger here" and "Reach out your hand and put it into my side. Stop doubting and believe."

Thomas' response was one of reverent worship. "My Lord and my God!" he exclaimed to Jesus. Thomas is worshipping Jesus as God. Note that Jesus did not rebuke Thomas for calling Him God and worshipping Him. He accepted it. In every other instance in the Bible (Old and New Testament) whenever someone falls at the feet of an angelic being or a man, he is immediately rebuked and corrected with the words "worship God only"[23] or "do not worship me—I am only a messenger." In the factual encounter between Thomas and the resurrected Christ, Jesus receives Thomas' worship because Jesus is God. He is God in human form.

Christian sources aren't the only ones which recognize the fact that Jesus claimed to be God. This is important because we are debunking the ridiculous claim that Jesus never claimed to be God and that it's only a much later invention of His sincere, but thoroughly misguided and superstitious followers who, overwhelmed by their love and respect for this great teacher, made a God out of Him at a much later date by inventing legends. Rubbish!

In modern trial law, there is a principle that gives strong weight to any evidence supporting your case that comes from your adversaries. This is based on the principle that your adversary is not likely to say or write anything that helps your case against him unless it's true. There's no reason or motive for your adversary to create evidence to favor your claims since his motivation would run counter to this. So, whatever your adversary says that's favorable to your cause is likely to be true. How is it possible to ever claim that Jesus was not understood to be divine by his earliest followers? By acknowledging in the earliest sources that Jesus was worshipped as "God," these hostile sources tacitly admit that this was not a later legend. It was not.

Don't believe what some of these other modern people write. When *The Da Vinci Code* first came out, I saw a woman reading it at the gym on an exercise machine and she cried out loud, "This is unbelievable!" I asked what she was reading. She said, "Did you know that Jesus was married?" I said to myself, "Oh no, where do I start?" She believed this nonsense simply because she knew nothing of Jesus to begin with. People will believe anything if they know nothing.

IT WAS THE BEST OF TIMES, IT WAS THE WORST OF TIMES

The death of Christ was a very strange event. It's the worst thing that ever happened, the worst crime, the most evil event in all of human history. It involves the torture and murder of a good man who helped people and healed people. It was a horrible injustice. Nobody reading the story could believe that it was justice to kill Jesus on that cross. He was good, kind and loving. It's sickening to read about how he was treated. Mel Gibson's film, *The Passion of the Christ*, pulls no punches in portraying the treatment of Jesus. It's one of the highest-grossing films of all time. The murder of Jesus was cruel and evil on an unimaginable scale. It was truly "the worst thing that ever happened" to a single person.

At the same time, the crucifixion of Jesus was the best thing that ever happened in the history of the world. How is this possible? Only God could pull this off. Isn't that remarkable? How could something simultaneously be the worst thing that ever happened and the best thing that ever happened? Here's why: if Jesus hadn't died on that cross, we would be in deep trouble. We would be dead in our sins and without hope. So, for us, it's the best thing that ever happened. It's simultaneously the worst and best thing that ever happened. Amazing.

Who killed Jesus? The Jews? The Romans? No, God killed Jesus. Jesus killed Jesus. Really. He offered up His own life for us. He essentially said, "Nobody takes my life. I offer it willingly."[24] It was a voluntary sacrificial act of His own will. This truth puts the entire sordid event into perspective.

The Scripture says He yielded up His spirit on the cross for our benefit. We know that from the Bible. Jesus died for us! It was foretold in advance by the prophets. And He rose again to demonstrate to us His power over death. Jesus is the only religious figure ever to have claimed to be risen from the dead. Moses, Muhammad, Buddha—all are buried, dead, and gone.

> The Scripture says He yielded up His spirit on the cross for our benefit.

CHOSEN, BUT FOR WHAT?

The Bible gives us a revelation of who God is. The Bible talks about the Jewish people as "the chosen people." That's true. Clearly, they are a chosen people, but I think the question that should be asked is, "Chosen for what?" Why did God choose them? For what purpose were they chosen? The Bible answers this question.

God picked a nation, Israel, and said in effect, "I'm going to use you as a blank canvas upon which to paint a portrait of myself." You see, you can't understand God apart from relationship with people. God can tell you what He's like, but it wouldn't make any sense in a vacuum. You need context to understand God. The only way for us to know what God is like is to see Him interact with His people. So, He took a group of people and He chose them. He chose them in order to interact with them and have those events recorded for all to know.

This was not because they were the wisest or best people. They were not the easiest people to deal with, the Bible says. It says they were a "very stubborn and stiff-necked people,"[25] essentially calling them perfect for what God is going to do. God needed a difficult nation to demonstrate His grace in the face of their rebellion and rejection of Him. God stretches out this blank canvas (the Jewish people), and in the Old Testament we have a portrait of who God is. We know His likes and dislikes, what He loves and what He hates. We see His grace. And ultimately, the Bible, from beginning to end, is a revelation of God. We have the revelation of God in words, the Scripture. There is great detail, for sure. But then we have a physical revelation of God in human form portrayed in Scripture: Jesus Christ, the god-man, a Jew.

PROPHECIES FULFILLED IN DETAIL BY JESUS

The very first prophecy concerning the Messiah is found in Genesis 3:15. It's in the Torah (the first book) and is generally agreed to have been written by Moses. It's referred to by scholars as the proto-prophecy. What does God say? He says, *"Eve, from the seed of a woman is going to come one who will crush the head of a serpent. He will bruise his heel, but he will crush his head."* We have some clues here. We know it's a man, and we know He is coming from a woman, and we know He is coming from the "seed of a woman." But a woman technically does not have "seed." There's a hint of something else here: the virgin birth. This passage also contains an ancient metaphor to indicate that, while the Messiah would be wounded ("heel" wound) by the adversary, the serpent would be dealt a mortal "head" wound.

This is referring to the crucifixion of Christ in which he was dead for three days, but thereby delivered a mortal wound (death blow) to Satan's stronghold on mankind. This certainly fits, since God gives this prophecy in the context of Adam and Eve's newly diagnosed sin problem. God is, in essence, saying that "you have been infected by sin, but don't worry, I've already prepared the antidote." The antidote is Jesus. He will crush evil.

Later on in Genesis, Moses writes that a prophet will arise, like Moses, from his own people. Now we have some clues as to who the Messiah will be. He will be a man. He will be from the seed of woman and he will be like Moses (meaning that he will be authoritative, with a unique relationship with God). Let's see what else develops in the Jewish Scriptures.

As the Scriptures unfold, we find out from Abraham that through his offspring "all nations of the earth are going to be blessed."[26] This prophecy indicates that the Messiah will come from Abraham and that it will be through Isaac and eventually Jacob (later renamed "Israel" from which the "Israelites" get their name). Here, we have proof that the Messiah would be Jewish, an "Israelite." Jesus was Jewish.

Now we know that something huge is going to happen through Abraham. We know the Messiah is going to be an Israelite, and we know he is coming out of Israel. But which of the twelve tribes? We are then told that "he'll be the Lion of the tribe of Judah"[27]—more clues here. When Jacob (Israel) blesses his twelve sons (which, in essence, became the twelve tribes of Israel), he singled out his son, Judah, as the one through whom the Messiah's line would come. He said to Judah, "The scepter will not depart from Judah,"[28] indicating that through Judah's line, the Messiah would come. The scepter indicates eternal kingship because it would "never depart." Jesus was Jewish, of the tribe of Judah.

The picture is getting clearer. We're getting more pieces to the puzzle. We read that the Messiah would be further narrowed down to one of Judah's descendants, King David. David's story is interesting because he became king through a most unlikely series of events. He was chosen by God, not because of physical stature or kingly bearing, but because of his heart.

When Samuel the prophet was told by God to anoint David (son of Jesse), he pretty much laughed in the face of everyone present because David was a most unlikely-looking candidate for a king. Samuel remarked, "surely God looks on the inside (and sees the heart) and not on the outside." I think a better translation might have been "God must be looking at his heart and not his outward appearance because there's not much going on here!" David, apparently, was not very impressive-looking. He was impressive on the inside, because the Bible says, "he was a man after God's own heart."[29]

This is the same David who had the courage to face a giant with a sling while the entire army of Israel cowered in terror. God was able to see this in advance, even though man (even a "holy" man like Samuel) was blinded to David's inner greatness. God was so impressed with David that he told him that a member of David's royal bloodline would sit on the throne forever! Forever means eternity. No dynasty, no matter how great, lasts forever. Only a spiritual dynasty can be eternal (another clue to the Messiah's identity unfolding, that Messiah would be "eternal God"). We find out His name shall be "wonderful counselor, mighty God, the Everlasting Father, the Prince of Peace." Is he going to be man or God? Is He going to be both? Sounds like both, since He is related to David (man), but will also be "mighty God" (divine). Jesus is Jewish, of the tribe of Judah, descended from David, and the eternal King.

We have evidence that Jesus descends from King David because Christ's genealogy is carefully recorded in the New Testament (Matthew, and again in Luke). The Jewish people are still waiting for their "messiah." One wonders how anyone could possibly prove he was descended from David today and claim to be "Messiah," since all birth and genealogy records of Jews prior to the first century were destroyed in 70 AD when the Second Temple was leveled by the Roman legions under General Titus Vespasian. This is the reason why modern Jews break a glass at a wedding. It's a solemn reminder, before the festivities begin, that we should not forget that the Temple (and the sacrificial altar) has not been around for almost 2,000 years and has yet to be rebuilt. Not only was the Temple destroyed, but everything in it as well, including all the records of the Jewish nation contained there.

Under Christian doctrine, there is no need for that Temple or that altar since Jesus, Himself, was the perfect and final sacrifice for our sin. This makes perfect sense, as it's hard to believe that sacrificing animals, as per the ancient Jewish Law of Atonement, would ever be sufficient to purge the sin of men. Only a man could suffice. He would have to be a perfect one for his sacrifice to be sufficient to cover the sins of all men. He would have to be eternal, God even, as well as a man to cover the sins of all humans. Only Jesus fits this bill.

There is an interesting story in the Torah about Abraham being asked to offer his son, his only begotten son Isaac, as a sacrifice to God. What a strange story! Why would God ask anyone, let alone one He favored, such as Abraham, to do such a thing? This is a brutal request. And this He asked of Abraham after He had already told him "through Isaac, all nations of the earth will be blessed." What an awkward position in which to be placed! Should Abraham obey this command? Or should he say "Hey, God! Remember that time you said all nations of the earth will be blessed through Isaac? Yeah, just reminding you in case you forgot...." Well Abraham trusted God so completely that he obeyed God's command and began the process of sacrificing his beloved son.

> **Under Christian doctrine, there is no need for that Temple or that altar since Jesus, Himself, was the perfect and final sacrifice for our sin.**

As Abraham treks up the mountain with his son to perform the sacrifice, Isaacs asks a strange question. He says, in essence, "Dad, we have the wood, we have the altar... but where's the sacrifice?" Apparently, Isaac was unaware that he was to be the sacrifice! It rips your heart out, this story.

Abraham's answer is interesting, particularly for the way it's phrased in Hebrew. He says, "The Lord will provide himself a sacrifice."[30] Wow! That surely can be taken several ways. Was God himself the sacrifice? Or did it merely mean that God would provide a suitable alternative to Isaac, a "substitutionary atonement," if you will? Whatever this means, it's clearly a statement by God that, though cryptic, is pregnant with meaning. It probably means both.

As they arrive at the place of the sacrifice, Abraham binds Isaac and places him on the altar. You must admit—considering that Abraham was an old man of 100-plus years—that Isaac had to submit voluntarily at this point, right? How else could this happen? Any resistance by Isaac ("Uh, Dad, what are you doing? Have you lost your mind?") would have resulted in Isaac's easy escape. But we have Isaac bound on the altar and Abraham raising his knife to heaven about to kill his beloved son when the Lord stops him. There, in the bush, "caught in a thicket," is a ram that Abraham sacrifices in place of his son. Isaac is "resurrected" in a sense, because he was spared at the eleventh hour.

What's interesting about all this is that we know exactly where this whole event happened. God told Abraham to take Isaac to Mount Moriah, to build an altar there, and sacrifice Isaac to God on the altar. After more than 3,500 years, we still call it Mount Moriah. It's in Jerusalem, and it's also called the Temple Mount. The Jewish Temples were built there to commemorate Abraham and Isaac's obedience to God.

There's another place on Mount Moriah that came to be called Golgotha. It's here where Jesus was crucified (sacrificed). Golgotha later came to be called Calvary. Coincidence? Hardly. Abraham's obedience was nothing short of acted-out prophecy of that which was to come. But, there's more—much more.

Read Isaiah 52:13–53:12 below and ask yourself a question: who is this passage of the Bible referring to?

THE SUFFERING AND GLORY OF THE SERVANT

Isaiah 52:13–15

13 See, my servant will act wisely;

he will be raised and lifted up and highly exalted.

14 Just as there were many who were appalled at him—

his appearance was so disfigured beyond that of any
human being
and his form marred beyond human likeness—
15 so he will sprinkle many nations,
and kings will shut their mouths because of him.
For what they were not told, they will see,
and what they have not heard, they will understand.

Isaiah 53:1–12
1 Who has believed our message
and to whom has the arm of the Lord been revealed?
2 He grew up before him like a tender shoot,
and like a root out of dry ground.
He had no beauty or majesty to attract us to him,
nothing in his appearance that we should desire him.
3 He was despised and rejected by mankind,
a man of suffering, and familiar with pain.
Like one from whom people hide their faces
he was despised, and we held him in low esteem.
4 Surely, he took up our pain
and bore our suffering,
yet we considered him punished by God,
stricken by him, and afflicted.
5 But he was pierced for our transgressions,
he was crushed for our iniquities;
the punishment that brought us peace was on him,
and by his wounds we are healed.

6 We all, like sheep, have gone astray,

each of us has turned to our own way;

and the Lord has laid on him

the iniquity of us all.

7 He was oppressed and afflicted,

yet he did not open his mouth;

he was led like a lamb to the slaughter,

and as a sheep before its shearers is silent,

so he did not open his mouth.

8 By oppression and judgment he was taken away.

Yet who of his generation protested?

For he was cut off from the land of the living;

for the transgression of my people he was punished.

9 He was assigned a grave with the wicked,

and with the rich in his death,

though he had done no violence,

nor was any deceit in his mouth.

10 Yet it was the Lord's will to crush him and cause him
to suffer,

and though the Lord makes his life an offering for sin,

he will see his offspring and prolong his days,

and the will of the Lord will prosper in his hand.

11 After he has suffered,

he will see the light of life and be satisfied;

by his knowledge my righteous servant will justify many,

and he will bear their iniquities.

12 Therefore I will give him a portion among the great,

and he will divide the spoils with the strong,
because he poured out his life unto death,
and was numbered with the transgressors.
For he bore the sin of many,
and made intercession for the transgressors.

This is describing Jesus of Nazareth. That's obvious to all who read this. He was "highly exalted." He was also "disfigured" and beaten so that "his form [was] marred beyond human likeness." He was "despised and rejected by man, a man of sorrows." He was the one who remained silent before Pilate and His accusers and did not say a word in his defense. He was buried in a rich man's tomb.

After the "suffering of his soul," he did see "the light of life" because he was resurrected. He "was numbered with the transgressors" because he was crucified between two criminals and suffered a "criminal's" death. Obviously, this refers to Jesus of Nazareth and His crucifixion, burial, and resurrection. It even says why this all happened: "for he bore the sins of many and made intercession for the transgressors."

What's the big deal? Some follower of Jesus must have written this, right? Wrong. This was written by the Jewish prophet Isaiah, approximately 750 years before Jesus was born! Staunchly Jewish apologists will tell you that this passage of Scripture refers to the nation of Israel.

Can any sincere interpretation of this come to that conclusion? Can Israel be considered sinless ("though he had done no violence, nor was any deceit in his mouth")? Is that a fair reading of Israel's history? If anything, Israel tested God's patience with its never-ending cycle of idolatry and oppression of the poor. Isaiah himself railed against this in his book, so he certainly didn't mean Israel. Israel was anything but sinless and innocent.

This can only be read as it reads. This is about a man: Messiah. A man who would be "crushed for our iniquities." Now we see that the Messiah—in addition to being a Jewish man, from the seed of a woman, from the tribe of

> **Here we have a perfect revelation that culminates, with miraculous focus, on Jesus Christ.**

Jacob and the lineage of David, with an eternal kingship— would also be rejected by his people and brutally killed. I think we're narrowing down the possibilities.

Flash-forward about 780 years from Isaiah's prophesy and Scripture starts to unroll until, finally, John the Baptist, a Jewish prophet, takes his bony finger and points at Jesus and says, "Behold, the Lamb of God who takes away the sin of the world." It doesn't get more specific than that!

Here we have a perfect revelation that culminates, with miraculous focus, on Jesus Christ. Then, if we want to know what God is like, we're able to look at Jesus from that point on. A child can do this! Jesus is loving, kind, forgiving, self-sacrificing, one who does not tolerate nonsense or hypocrisy. The Bible—from beginning to end, when all is said and done, when all the lectures are completed, when all the evidence is put forth—is, in word form, a portrait of our Savior, Jesus Christ.

The Bible is, essentially, information at its core. That's the importance of the Bible. It's informational truth about God. It's truth about man's condition. "For the word of God is alive and active. Sharper than any double-edged sword, it penetrates even to dividing soul and spirit, joints and marrow; it judges the thoughts and attitudes of the heart" (Hebrews 4:12). As it says about itself, the word of God is alive and "powerful" (KJV translation). It's alive and powerful because truth is alive and powerful. Truth illuminates. It keeps one from stumbling about in the dark. God did not want us to remain in the dark about who He is, what He desires from us, and about what our condition is. He revealed this to us in the form of the Bible, a revelation about Himself for all of the world to see, to process and to comprehend. We must, then, also act upon it.

COMPELLING EVIDENCE TO CONSIDER THE TESTIMONY OF THE BIBLE

The Bible has clearly had a strong impact on the world. Here is only a partial list of things that exist today or have altered human history because of events recorded in the Bible.

1. The existence today, some 2,000 years later, of 2.2 billion people who gather together every week to celebrate a resurrected Jesus Christ, crucified under the ancient Roman governor, Pontius Pilate.
2. The fact that the earliest Christians, who were Jews, willingly changed their sacred Sabbath day from a Saturday (the last day of the week) to a Sunday (the first day, now the "Lord's day").
3. The existence of countless works of art, songs, museums, cathedrals, hospitals, orphanages, schools, and churches which exist to advance healing, education, and good in the name of Jesus.
4. The existence of a written book called the Bible, compiled over 1,500 years, which is the foundation

for Western civilization and still the bestseller every year for 2,000 years and the most translated and copied book of all time.

5. The conversion in modern times, by persuasion and not force, of 30,000 people per day in China, often at great personal cost and no immediate earthly benefit.

6. The present-day conversion of Muslims in countries hostile to Christianity in exchange for torture and sacrifice of their lives.

7. The evidence of the testimony of countless changed lives of people who are consistently being transformed from drug addicts and otherwise broken, unproductive beings into successful and effective citizens.

8. The innumerable prophecies of the Bible fulfilled in minute detail, predicted centuries in advance, which authenticate the Bible as what it claims to be: the Word of God. The Bible claims to be the Word of God over 2,000 times.

9. The amazing examples of forgiveness extended by people to their persecutors and tormentors because the Bible teaches it. One notable example is Corrie ten Boom, who forgave the Nazi guard from the concentration camp where she was severely abused and where her sister died alongside her during WWII. This true story was

made into a movie called *The Hiding Place* in the 1970s.

10. The ending of slavery in the Roman Empire due to the influence of Christianity and the Bible.

11. The ending of slavery in the entire British Empire by the work of William Wilberforce, a committed Christian member of Parliament who sacrificed himself and his chance to be prime minister for this cause.

12. The recorded witness of the Apostles to the risen Christ and to the miracles and life of Jesus, eyewitnesses who, despite being tortured to death, never recanted their testimony, but went joyfully to their death proclaiming "Jesus is Lord."

13. The destruction of the Jewish Temple in 70 AD predicted by Jesus (ending animal sacrifices), forever changing the nature of Judaism from an animal "sacrificial" religion to its modern form. This fits perfectly with the crucifixion of Jesus as the one and only true sacrifice for sin as recorded in the Bible as having been made for all time.

14. The discovery of the Dead Sea Scrolls, demonstrating no corruption in the biblical text being transmitted over millennia.

15. The incredibly generous acts of people motivated by biblical values (Jews and Christians) who give millions of dollars to causes advanced by the

Bible such as medicine, healing, and caregiving to others, whether or not they deserve it.

16. The existence of countless laws mirrored on the morality of the Bible, such as "do not steal" "do not murder," and "do not give false testimony." These laws are necessary for a just and good society.

17. The existence of a remarkably consistent code of human morality over time, place, and various cultures consistent with what is written in the Bible, pointing to an objective moral law that transcends human beings and is authored by a Creator.

18. The proliferation of thousands of Biblical quotes and principles used commonly in everyday speech by millions of people daily, such as "my brother's keeper," "fight the good fight," "fly in the ointment," and "old as the hills."

19. The everyday people that have found timeless wisdom in the Bible for successful, productive, and fulfilled living.

20. The restoration of broken relationships and marriages through biblical counseling and biblical principles. One example is Rev. Joyce Meyers who forgave her father who incestuously raped her as a young girl. She forgave him and later baptized him into the faith.[1]

21. The desire of man for the "other-worldly" in seeking to find meaning that transcends his own existence.

The quest for the eternal that is a common human endeavor as evidenced by the fact that humans are inherently religious. God has placed eternity in the heart of man (Eccl 3:11).

22. The fact that all humans "worship" something. If not the Creator God, then an idol of some type: a sports figure, a musician or musical group, money, or some other person or pet. Man was made with an inclination to worship, as taught in the Bible.

23. The constant tension between good and evil and the struggle that characterizes human existence in which we are free to choose between the two. The fact that human beings are capable of both monstrous evil and great good, as taught in the Bible.

24. The existence of the English language itself, which would look much different except for the efforts of William Tyndale (called the "architect of the English language"). Tyndale invented many words in this language while translating the Bible.

25. The existence of non-violent protests, based on appeals to justice and objective morality as taught in the Bible, by people such as Rev. Martin Luther King, Jr., who shamed oppressors into doing the right thing.

26. The life and ministry of Jesus of Nazareth, the most remarkable person who ever lived, as recorded in

the Bible. Simultaneously worshipped and scorned, He is the most divisive and yet most revered figure of the human race. He is believed by Christians to be God manifest in human form and by Muslims to be a prophet who will someday return to Earth. Thus, fully two-thirds of the world's people believe Him to be someone supernatural, special, and amazing, two thousand years after he walked the earth. Jesus lived a perfect and sinless life in service to others. He elevated the meek and humbled the mighty. He is merciful to the common sinner, yet railed angrily against the religious hypocrites. His name is used by His followers to bless people and as a curse word by others. He is the only major world figure and the only religious leader who ever claimed to have risen bodily from death. People have and continue to willingly die to follow Him. He is nothing short of wonderful to those who know Him.

CONCLUSION TO THE MATTER

The Bible also reveals to us our innermost thoughts. This may make us uncomfortable at times. In the long run, however, it helps us to get a grip on who we are and what we're about. It brings healing in much the same way that a medicine often tastes bad or is difficult to swallow even while it's beneficial. Usually, the sicker we are, the stronger the medicine we need.

Or, to change metaphors, the Bible points us in the right direction like a road map. That direction is toward God, not away from Him. Some of us have wandered very far from God. If you're away from God, or your life is pointing in the wrong direction, the sooner you change direction, the better. It may give us temporary solace to hide from God, or to run farther away when our attitudes and our thoughts differ so much from His, but to what end? How could that ever benefit us? If we run from God, what exactly are we running toward? The opposite can't be good. This is a valid question. One can only avoid the truth for so long and then it has a way of biting us hard in the back. No amount of pretending or avoidance behavior will change reality, as much as we would like to believe otherwise. If you want to question the Bible, go ahead. If you want to debate it, go ahead. If you want to try to disprove it, try! But don't ignore it. You ignore it at your own peril. It's far too important to be ignored. It claims too much importance to be ignored. It claims to be the very words of God. It follows, then, that it either is or it isn't! And if it is, then that is a reality that must be confronted directly, don't you think?

Much of what you hear or what people believe about God today is the product of whim or wishful thinking. It's created out of a desire for an easier concept of God and is man's vain attempt to avoid the pain that being in conflict with God often causes. But God can't be tamed despite man's best efforts to do so. God may be good, but he is not tame. He thinks and acts in ways that are far above our ways and thoughts. "For my thoughts are not your thoughts, neither are your ways my ways," declares the LORD in Isaiah 55:8. Yet, we continually try to re-invent God. But in the end, it's really only an attempt to create Him in our own image. We try to "create" a God that we can live with, one that doesn't make us too uncomfortable or demand too much of us. Is this wise? You be the judge. Get to know God as He really is, as the many ancients have witnessed and declared and has been written down for posterity in the Bible. Let the Bible inform you. Let the Bible speak to you. So, rather than create your own opinions about God out of thin air, why not just accept and believe what God has revealed about Himself? Analyze it and critique it if you like, but at least give it a fair chance.

That's the true importance of the Bible. It is truth about God, mankind, and our problems. It's the truth from the various people who were contemplative in the wilderness under the stars, those who heard from God before the conveniences and distractions of modern life created so much noise. It's the truth about God from witnesses who were in an actual position to know the things written in its pages. It's the truth about God from people who were witnesses to the life, the power, the words of wisdom, and the resurrection of Jesus Christ.

God is still speaking today. He has not stopped. He is alive and well and interactive. The question is, are we listening? How much time do you spend praying and seeking God? How many people are truly contemplative about these things today? How many people today are asking the big questions of life? Who is God? Who am I? Where did I come from? Where am I going? What is my purpose in life? What does God want from me? Yet, God is still there actively communicating to mankind. He is speaking to the hearts and minds of people today. He is using people today to accomplish his purposes.

So, what side are you on? Are you on the side of truth? Just as the Bible contains a harmonious testimony about God from various sources, who He is and what

He's like, any further communications from God will be consistent with that. Anything else is false teaching. God will not contradict himself. God is not schizophrenic. His character is immutable and does not change. Times may change. Attitudes may change. People may change, but God is consistent. We have the Bible as the standard by which to judge any further communications from God. The Bible is to theology (the study of God) like the American Constitution is to the jurisprudence of the United States. It is the standard by which to judge any future laws. If a law violates the Constitution, it is thrown out as "unconstitutional." It must conform to the standard of the Constitution or it's invalid.[1]

Human beings have been remarkably consistent over time in how they behave such that there is "nothing new under the sun,"[2] as Solomon famously said. "What has been will be again, what has been done will be done again; there is nothing new under the sun," is the full quote. This was written approximately 950 B.C., almost 3,000 years ago. Truth has no statute of limitations. Basic human nature has not changed, even if attitudes about it have. What was true then is still true today, and this underscores the importance of the Bible. Our response to truth may be different, but the truth itself remains.

Similarly, any future "revelation" about God or the condition of man must be consistent with the Bible or it is "unbiblical" ("unconstitutional") and should be discarded. The Bible is the standard.

"Now all has been heard; here is the conclusion of the matter: Fear God and keep His commandments, for this is the duty of all mankind."[3] What are His commandments? What are His gifts? What are His precious promises to us? Read the Bible to find out.

ABOUT THE AUTHOR

Daniel P. Buttafuoco is a trial lawyer who has tried hundreds of jury and non-jury trials over the course of a 35-year career representing injury and malpractice victims. His office currently has over 600 cases pending in various states. He and his associates have successfully concluded over 100 separate cases for over one million dollars each. Altogether, his offices have nearly half a billion dollars in settled and paid cases.

A member of the Million Dollar Advocates Forum and other prestigious trial lawyer groups.

Graduate of Hofstra University's New College with a BA in psychology.

Graduate of Hofstra Law School

Master's Degree (of professional studies) in Theology from Alliance Theological Seminary with an emphasis in Christian Apologetics.

Formerly an adjunct volunteer professor of the National Institute of Trial Advocacy's "Trial techniques" course, which would put law school graduates and practicing lawyers through a rigorous training program of trial skills and techniques.

Board certified in Civil Trial Advocacy and Pre-trial advocacy by the National Board of Trial Advocacy

Mr. Buttafuoco wrote and graded the qualifying examination for the National Board of Trial Advocacy (civil part) in 1990

A Church Elder for 25 years.

Mr. Buttafuoco is a regular lecturer and speaker at various schools, institutions and churches of all denominations, including the Billy Graham Library and Moody Theological Seminary.

Founder and President of the Historical Bible Society, a not for profit organization that collects, displays, and preserves rare and ancient Bibles for public and private education.

ACKNOWLEDGMENTS

I would like to thank Rob Taormina and Sam Mikhail for their help and encouragement in getting out the message of the Historical Bible Society. They have appeared with me and supported me at so many events that I cannot possibly thank them enough. They were inspirational to this venture.

Special thanks also to Phil Abbruscato, a budding young lawyer with tremendous potential who assisted in the editing of this book and endnotes. He handled the things I simply did not have the time to do in the middle of my busy law practice and he did it with wisdom and precision.

In addition, I would like to thank my assistant, Danielle Terpis-Pollera, who typed seemingly endless drafts of this book during normal work hours in addition to the other very important work she does for my law firm.

Finally, I would like to thank all of those open-minded people who sincerely are searching for spiritual answers to the big questions in life.

The Bible contains those answers.

END NOTES

Introduction
1 Luke 1:1–4
2 "What is Apologetics?" https://bible.org/seriespage/2-what-apologetics.

Exhibit A
1 Matthew 6:9–13
2 "What does it mean for us to call God our Father?" *Ligonier* Ministries, http://www.ligonier.org/learn/qas/what-does-it-mean-us-call-god-our-father.
3 "Tyndale Bible History," http://www.william-tyndale.com/tyndale-bible-history.html.
4 David Streater, "William Tyndale (1494–1536)—Architect of The English Reformation," *Church Society* (Issue Spring 1994 No. 52), http://archive.churchsociety.org/crossway/documents/Cway_052_Streater-Tyndale.pdf.
5 "Tyndale Bible History" http://www.william-tyndale.com/tyndale-bible-history.html.
6 "The Forbidden Book," New Liberty Videos.
7 Evan Andrews, "7 Things You May Not Know About the Gutenberg Bible" *History*, http://www.history.com/news/7-things-you-may-not-know-about-the-gutenberg-bible
8 "History of The Gutenberg Bible" http://www.gutenberg-bible.com/history.html.
9 "The Bible vs. Mao: A "Best Guess" of the Top 25 Bestselling Books of All Time" *Growth Markets* (2010), http://publishingperspectives.com/2010/09/top-25-bestselling-books-of-all-time/.
10 "Growth of the Church" *The Traveling Team* (2015), http://www.thetravelingteam.org/articles/growth-of-the-church.
11 Acts 17:6

12 Matthew 7:24
13 Matthew 7:12
14 "English Bible History," http://www.greatsite.com/
    timeline-english-bible-history/.
15 *Id.*
16 Barbara Tuchman, *The March of Folly (from Troy to
    Vietnam)* (Alfred A. Knopf, NY 1984).
17 Michael J. Walsh, *The Lives of the Popes,* (Salamander
    Books Ltd., 1998).
18 "English Bible History," http://www.greatsite.com/
    timeline-english-bible-history/.
19 *Id.*
20 Slaves, in ancient times, were mostly prisoners of war that
    were not killed. They were survivors of battles and
    conflicts.
21 Luke 4:16–20
22 John 1:14
23 Karl Marx, *A Contribution to the Critique of Hegel's
    Philosophy of Right* (1843).
24 Mark 12:17
25 Rick Warren, *The Purpose Driven Life* (Grand Rapids,
    MI: Zondervan, 2002).
26 Matthew 9:27–31
27 John 11:1–44
28 Matthew 14:13–21
29 Mark 2:1–12
30 Matthew 5, 6 and 7
31 Luke 24:1–9
32 John 20:27
33 John 21:1–15

Exhibit B

1 "English Bible History," http://www.greatsite.com/
   timeline-english-bible-history/.
2 *Id.*
3 *Id.*
4 John 2:1–11
5 Matthew 8:27
6 Matthew 14:22–34
7 John 11:38–44
8 Mark 11: 12–21

9 Acts 2:22–32
10 Mark 16:15
11 "The Motives of Judas in Betraying Jesus,"
    Bible Hub, http://biblehub.com/library/neander/
    the_life_of_jesus_christ_in_its_historical_connexion/
    section_264_the_motives_of.htm.
12 John 18:36
13 Matthew 27:4
14 Matthew 27:1–10
15 Joan Oakes, "What is the evidence that Peter was
    crucified upside down in Rome?" *Evidence for
    Christianity* (2010), http://evidenceforchristianity.org/
    what-is-the-evidence-that-peter-was-crucified-upside-
    down-in-rome/.
16 Hebrews 11:37
17 2 Peter 1:16
18 *Id.*
19 1 John 1:1–4
20 *Apologeticus*, 50, s. 13 (Often quoted as "The blood of
    the martyrs is the seed of the church"). Variant
    translations include, "As often as we are mown down
    by you, the more we grow in numbers; the blood of the
    Christians is the seed" and "The blood of the Martyrs is
    the seed of Christians." Tertullian is also the one to whom
    we attribute the quote "Out of the frying pan into the f
    ire." *De Carne Christi*, 6 (The Roman version translates to
    "Out of the lime-kiln into the coal-furnace").
21 Maulana Hafiz Sher Mohammad, "The Death of Jesus
    according to Islamic sources" http://www.muslim.org/
    islam/deathj-6.htm.
22 "Time line of Christianity and Islam" *Agape Bible Study*,
    http://www.agapebiblestudy.com/charts/Time%20
    Line%20of%20Christianity%20and%20Islam.htm.
    "Before this, you did not read any book, nor did
    you write anything with your hands." Surah 29:48;
    All historians are unanimous that the Prophet was an
    unlettered man who had never known books or
    teachers and never learned how to write. "Prophet
    Muhammad (S) was Unlettered" *Al-Islam.org* (2017)
    https://www.al-islam.org/authenticity-
    Qur'an-shaykh-muslim-bhanji/prophet-muhammad
    -was-unlettered.

23 John 19:26
24 John 20:31
25 1 John 1:1–3
26 Acts 2:32
27 e.g. Acts 20:5, 6
28 Acts 2:41
29 John 20:24–27
30 Hebrews 12:2
31 Mark 3:20, 21
32 1 Corinthians 15:7
33 Exodus 20:8
34 Revelation 1:10
35 Acts 20:7
36 "What Makes the Bible So Special?" *Josh McDowell Ministry*, http://www.josh.org/resources/apologetics/answering-skeptics/what-makes-the-bible-so-special/.
37 Isaiah 44:6
38 Bodie Hodge, "Harvard, Yale, Princeton, Oxford—Once Christian?" *Answers in Genesis* (2007), https://answersingenesis.org/christianity/harvard-yale-princeton-oxford-once-christian/
39 William Grassie, *The Blog*, HUFFINGTON POST (May 6, 2013) (quoting an often-quoted saying).
40 Nancy Pearcey, "The Soul of Science" (1994).

Exhibit C

1 "What is the difference between exegesis and eisegesis?" https://www.gotquestions.org/exegesis-eisegesis.html.
2 2 Peter 1:20
3 Walter C. Kaiser, Jr, "How Has Archaeology Corroborated the Bible?" (2017) https://billygraham.org/decision-magazine/february-2017/archaeology-corroborated-bible/.
4 *Id.*
5 Norman Geisler, "Tired, Trustworthy, and True" *Decision Magazine* (2017).
6 *Id.*
7 Ann Wroe, "Historical Notes: Pontius Pilate: a name set in stone" *Independent* (1999), http://www.independent.co.uk/news/people/historical-notes-pontius-pilate-a-name-set-in-stone-1084786.html.

8 Archibald Sayce, "The Hittites" (1888).

9 Fᴇᴅ. R. Eᴠɪᴅ. 803.

10 "English Bible History: Timeline of how we got the English Bible" http://www.greatsite.com/ timeline-english-bible-history/.

11 Brendan Breed "What Are the Earliest Versions and Translations of the Bible?" *Bible Odyssey* (2017), http:// www.bibleodyssey.org/tools/bible-basics/what-are-the-earliest-versions-and-translations-of-the-bible.aspx.

12 *Id.*

13 "The Magdalen Papyrus P64: possibly the earliest known fragments of the New Testament (or of a book!)" *Magdalen College* (2013), http://www.magd. ox.ac.uk/libraries-and-archives/treasure-of-the-month/ news/magdalen-papyrus/.

14 "Homer Before Print" https://www.lib.uchicago.edu /e/webexhibits/homerinprint/preprint.html

15 David B. Wallace, "The Majority Text and the Original Text: Are They Identical?" *Bible.org* (2004), https://bible.org/ article/majority-text-and-original-text-are-they-identical.

16 Translations available at: http://biblehub.com/ john/3-16.htm.

17 Numbers 21:4–9

18 J. Warner Wallace, "Can We Construct The Entire New Testament From the Writings of the Church Fathers?" *Cold-Case Christianity with J. Warner Wallace* (2016), http://coldcasechristianity.com/2016/can-we-construct-the-entire-new-testament-from-the-writings-of-the-church-fathers/.

19 Edward D. Gravely, "The Text Critical Sigla in Codex Vaticanus" (2009).

20 Philip Comfort, *Essential Guide to Bible Versions* (Tyndale House Publishers, Inc., 2000), 151.

21 Acts 13:22

22 2 Samuel 11

23 Matthew 26:33

24 Luke 22:34

25 Galatians 2:11–13

26 Mark 16:9

27 Jim Campbell, *The Stories of the Old Testament* (Loyola Press, 2007), 114.

28 Julian Cheatle, "Nostradamus election prediction 2016: Clinton to be president not Trump," *Monsters & Critics* (2016), http://www.monstersandcritics.com/smallscreen/nostradamus-election-prediction-2016-clinton-to-be-president-not-trump/.

29 "Septuagint—What is It?" http://www.septuagint.net.

30 Mark 13:2

31 Josephus' account appears in: Cornfield, Gaalya ed., Josephus, The Jewish War (1982); Duruy, Victor, History of Rome vol. V (1883).

32 Josephus, "History of the Jews."

33 Hebrews 10:4

34 "353 Prophecies Fulfilled in Jesus Christ," *According to the Scriptures*, http://www.accordingtothescriptures.org/prophecy/353prophecies.html.

35 Matthew 2:1–6

36 John 1:46

37 Hugh J. Schonfield, *The Passover Plot* (London: Macdonald and Jane's, 1974).

38 Matthew 1:1–17; Luke 3:23–38

Exhibit D

1 Psalm 34:8

2 Acts 26:10

3 His own recitation of his credentials is as follows: "If someone else thinks they have reasons to put confidence in the flesh I have more: circumcised on the eighth day, of the people of Israel, of the tribe of Benjamin, a Hebrew of Hebrews; in regard to the law, a Pharisee; as for zeal, persecuting the church; as for righteousness based on the law, faultless." Philippians 3:4–6

4 Galatians 1:13, 14

5 Acts 9:2

6 Acts 26:9

7 Acts 22:1–21

8 John 3:1–21

9 Mark 9:2–9

10 2 Peter 1:16

11 John 20:31

12 John 6:68

13 1 Corinthians 14:34

14 Galatians 3:28

15 "Conversion of St. Augustine" *Midwest Augustinians,* https://www.midwestaugustinians.org/conversion-of-st-augustine/.

16 *Id.*

17 *Id.*

18 Chris Armstrong, "The Amazingly Graced Life of John Newton" *Christianity Today,* (2004) http://www.christianitytoday.com/history/issues/issue-81/amazingly-graced-life-of-john-newton.html.

19 *Id.*

20 *Id.*

21 *Id.*

22 Diane Severance, "John Newton Discovered Amazing Grace," *Christianity.com,* http://www.christianity.com/church/church-history/timeline/1701-1800/john-newton-discovered-amazing-grace-11630253.html.

23 *Id.*

24 *Id.*

25 "John Newton, Reformed slave trader," *Christianity Today,* http://www.christianitytoday.com/history/people/pastorsandpreachers/john-newton.html.

26 Al Rogers, "Amazing Grace: The Story of John Newton," http://www.anointedlinks.com/amazing_grace.html.

27 *Id.*

28 "History of Teen Challenge," *Teen Challenge* https://teenchallenge.cc/history-of-teen-challenge/

29 *Id.*

30 Nicky Cruz, *Run Baby Run* (Plainfield, NJ: *Logos International,* 1968).

31 Stephen V. Monsma, "Are Faith-Based Programs More Effective?" *The Center for Public Justice* (2001), https://www.cpjustice.org/public/page/content/faith_based_programs.

32 *Id.*

33 Nabeel Qureshi, "Crossing Over: An Intellectual and Spiritual Journey from Islam to Christianity," http://www.answering-islam.org/Authors/Qureshi/testimony.htm.

34 *Id.*

35 *Id.*

36 Nabeel Qureshi, "Christ Called Me Off the Minaret," *Christianity Today* (2014), http://www.christianitytoday.com/ct/2014/january-february/christ-called-me-off-minaret.html?start=2

37 Michael J Kruger, "Is the Bible the Word of God?" *Table Talk Magazine* (2017) https://tabletalkmagazine.com/article/2017/08/is-the-bible-the-word-of-god/.

Exhibit E

1 "Ignorance of Scripture is Ignorance of Christ—Jerome." https://www.crossroadsinitiative.com/media/articles/ignorance-of-scripture-is-ignorance-of-christ-st-jerome/

2 Kenneth Berding, "The Crisis of Biblical Illiteracy and what we can do about it" *Decision Magazine* (2014).

3 C.S. Lewis, *Mere Christianity* (Geoffrey Bless, 1952),55–56.

4 Pliny, *Letters* 10.96–97.

5 John 5:39

6 Isaiah 9:6

7 Matthew 12:22–37

8 John 5:30–40

9 Deuteronomy 6:4–9

10 John 10:33

11 Matthew 28:18

12 Daniel 7:13, 14

13 Mark 2:2–5

14 Mark 2:6,7

15 Mark 2:11

16 Mark 2:28

17 Mark 3:22

18 Matthew 12:25

19 John 14:9

20 John 8:58

21 Exodus 3:13

22 John 10:30

23 Revelation 22:9

24 John 10:18

25 Exodus 32:9

26 Genesis 22:18

27 Genesis 49:8–21

28 Genesis 49:10

29 Act 13:22

30 Genesis 22:8

Compelling Evidence to Consider the Testimony of the Bible
1 Mary Hutchinson, *Joyce Meyer Leads Her Father to Faith*, CHARISMA MAGAZINE, (APRIL 30, 2002).

Conclusion to the Matter
1 Sadly, this constancy has been weakened these days by the theory that the United States Constitution is a "living breathing document" that can be changed to fit the times.
2 Ecclesiastes 1:9
3 Ecclesiastes 12:13

NOTES